Improving Agile
Retrospectives

Pearson Addison-Wesley
Signature Series

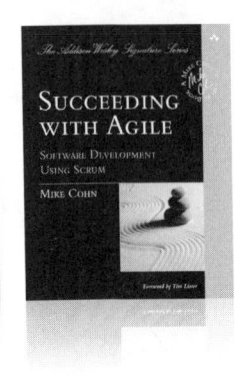

Visit informit.com/awss/cohn **for a complete list of available publications.**

The Pearson Addison-Wesley Signature Series provides readers with practical and authoritative information on the latest trends in modern technology for computer professionals. The series is based on one simple premise: great books come from great authors.

Books in the Mike Cohn Signature series are personally chosen by Cohn, a founder of the Agile Alliance and highly regarded Agile expert and author. Mike's signature ensures that he has worked closely with authors to define topic coverage, book scope, critical content, and overall uniqueness. The expert signatures also symbolize a promise to our readers: you are reading a future classic.

Make sure to connect with us!
informit.com/socialconnect

Improving Agile Retrospectives

Helping Teams Become More Efficient

Marc Loeffler

Translated from German by
Eamonn O'Leary

♦Addison-Wesley

Boston • Columbus • Indianapolis • New York • San Francisco
Amsterdam • Cape Town • Dubai • London • Madrid • Milan
Munich • Paris • Montreal • Toronto • Delhi • Mexico City
São Paulo • Sydney • Hong Kong • Seoul • Singapore
Taipei • Tokyo

Editor-in-Chief: Mark Taub
Executive Editor: Chris Guzikowski
Development Editor: Chris Zahn
Managing Editor: Sandra Schroeder
Senior Project Editor: Lori Lyons
Copy Editor: Paula Lowell
Indexer: Erika Millen
Proofreader: H S Rupa
Editorial Assistant: Courtney Martin
Cover Designer: Chuti Prasertsith
Compositor: codeMantra

Many of the designations used by manufacturers and sellers to distinguish their products are claimed as trademarks. Where those designations appear in this book, and the publisher was aware of a trademark claim, the designations have been printed with initial capital letters or in all capitals.

The author and publisher have taken care in the preparation of this book, but make no expressed or implied warranty of any kind and assume no responsibility for errors or omissions. No liability is assumed for incidental or consequential damages in connection with or arising out of the use of the information or programs contained herein.

For information about buying this title in bulk quantities, or for special sales opportunities (which may include electronic versions; custom cover designs; and content particular to your business, training goals, marketing focus, or branding interests), please contact our corporate sales department at corpsales@pearsoned.com or (800) 382-3419.

For government sales inquiries, please contact governmentsales@pearsoned.com.

For questions about sales outside the U.S., please contact intlcs@pearson.com.

Visit us on the Web: informit.com/aw

Library of Congress Control Number: 2017959642

Copyright © 2018 Pearson Education, Inc.

All rights reserved. Printed in the United States of America. This publication is protected by copyright, and permission must be obtained from the publisher prior to any prohibited reproduction, storage in a retrieval system, or transmission in any form or by any means, electronic, mechanical, photocopying, recording, or likewise. For information regarding permissions, request forms, and the appropriate contacts within the Pearson Education Global Rights & Permissions Department, please visit www.pearsoned.com/permissions/.

ISBN-13: 978-0-13-467834-4
ISBN-10: 0-13-467834-6

1 17

To mom and dad.

Contents at a Glance

	Foreword by Jutta Eckstein	xv
	Preface	xix
	Acknowledgments	xxi
	About the Author	xxiii
Chapter 1	Retrospectives 101	1
Chapter 2	Preparing Retrospectives	31
Chapter 3	The First Retrospective	43
Chapter 4	The Retrospective Facilitator	55
Chapter 5	From the Metaphor to the Retrospective	91
Chapter 6	Systemic Retrospectives	119
Chapter 7	Solution-Focused Retrospectives	155
Chapter 8	Distributed Retrospectives	179
Chapter 9	Alternative Approaches	193
Chapter 10	Typical Problems and Pitfalls	201
Chapter 11	Change Management	215
	Index	231

Contents

Foreword by Jutta Eckstein xv

Preface xix

Acknowledgments xxi

About the Author xxiii

Chapter 1 Retrospectives 101 1
    1.1 What Is a Retrospective? 1
    1.2 New Year's Eve Retrospective 6
    1.3 The Retrospective Phase Model 8
        1.3.1 Phase 1: Set the Stage 9
        1.3.2 Phase 2: Check Hypothesis 12
        1.3.3 Phase 3: Gather Data 13
        1.3.4 Phase 4: Generate Insights 16
        1.3.5 Phase 5: Define Experiments 17
        1.3.6 Phase 6: Closing 19
    1.4 Finding Activities for Each of the Phases 22
        1.4.1 Agile Retrospectives Book 23
        1.4.2 Retromat 23
        1.4.3 Retrospective Wiki 24
        1.4.4 Tasty Cupcakes 24
        1.4.5 Gamestorming 25
    1.5 The Prime Directive 26
    Summary 28

Chapter 2 Preparing Retrospectives 31
    2.1 Preparation 31
        2.1.1 What Period of Time Should Be Discussed? 31
        2.1.2 Who Should Take Part? 32
        2.1.3 Is There a Topic? 33
    2.2 The Right Time, the Right Place 34
    2.3 The Right Material 36
        2.3.1 The Right Markers 36
        2.3.2 The Right Sticky notes 37
        2.3.3 The Right Flipchart Paper 38

	2.4 Food	39
	2.5 The Agenda	40
	Summary	42
Chapter 3	**The First Retrospective**	**43**
	3.1 Preparation	43
	3.2 Set the Stage: Car Comparison	45
	3.3 Gather Data	46
	3.4 Generate Insights: 5 Whys	49
	3.5 Define Next Experiments: Brainstorming	50
	3.6 Closing: ROTI	53
	Summary	53
Chapter 4	**The Retrospective Facilitator**	**55**
	4.1 How Do I Become a Good Facilitator?	55
	4.1.1 Respect Different Communication Styles	58
	4.1.2 Paraphrasing	59
	4.1.3 Support Participants	59
	4.1.4 Stacking	60
	4.1.5 Encourage	61
	4.1.6 Feedback Emotion	61
	4.1.7 Intended Silence	62
	4.1.8 Listen for Common Ground	63
	4.2 Visual Facilitation	63
	4.2.1 The 1×1 of Visual Structure	64
	4.3 Visual Retrospectives	71
	4.3.1 The Speedboat Retrospective	71
	4.3.2 Trading Cards	74
	4.3.3 Perfection Game	76
	4.3.4 Force Field Analysis	78
	4.3.5 Sources of Inspiration for Visual Facilitation	80
	4.4 Internal or External	81
	4.4.1 Tips for Internal Facilitators	83
	4.4.2 External Facilitators	85
	4.5 After the Retro Is Before the Retro	87
	Summary	88
Chapter 5	**From the Metaphor to the Retrospective**	**91**
	5.1 The Orchestra Retrospective	93
	5.1.1 Set the Stage	94
	5.1.2 Gather Data	95

- 5.1.3 Generate Insights 97
- 5.1.4 Define Experiments and Hypothesis 98
- 5.1.5 Closing 99
- 5.2 The Soccer Retrospective 99
  - 5.2.1 Preparation 100
  - 5.2.2 Set the Stage 100
  - 5.2.3 Gather Data 101
  - 5.2.4 Generating Insights 102
  - 5.2.5 Define Next Experiments and Hypothesis 102
  - 5.2.6 Closing 103
- 5.3 The Train Retrospective 103
  - 5.3.1 Set the Stage 103
  - 5.3.2 Gather Data 104
  - 5.3.3 Generate Insights 105
  - 5.3.4 Define Experiments and Hypothesis 106
  - 5.3.5 Closing 107
- 5.4 The Kitchen Retrospective 107
  - 5.4.1 Set the Stage 107
  - 5.4.2 Gather Data 108
  - 5.4.3 Generate Insights 109
  - 5.4.4 Define Experiments and Hypothesis 111
  - 5.4.5 Closing 111
- 5.5 The Pirate Retrospective 111
  - 5.5.1 Set the Stage 112
  - 5.5.2 Gather Data 113
  - 5.5.3 Generate Insights 114
  - 5.5.4 Define Experiments and Hypothesis 115
  - 5.5.5 Closing 116
- Summary 117

Chapter 6 Systemic Retrospectives 119
- 6.1 Systems 120
  - 6.1.1 Static and Dynamic 122
  - 6.1.2 Complicated and Complex 122
- 6.2 System Thinking 124
  - 6.2.1 Causal Loop Diagrams 125
  - 6.2.2 Current Reality Tree 137
  - 6.2.3 Limitations of System Thinking 142

6.3 Complexity Thinking 143
    6.3.1 Martie—The Management 3.0 Model 144
    6.3.2 The ABIDE Model 147
Summary 152

Chapter 7   Solution-Focused Retrospectives 155

7.1 The Solution-Focused Approach 156
    7.1.1 Problem Talk Creates Problems,
           Solution Talk Creates Solutions 156
    7.1.2 Focus on the Better Future 157
    7.1.3 No Problem Happens All the Time;
           There Are Always Exceptions That Can
           Be Utilized 158
    7.1.4 If It Works, Do More of It 159
    7.1.5 If It's Not Working, Do Something Different 160
    7.1.6 Small Steps Can Lead to Big Changes 161
    7.1.7 Focus on Strength and Skills 161
    7.1.8 Understand and Trust That Each Person
           Is an Expert in His or Her Own Situation 162
    7.1.9 Keep the Attitude of Not Knowing 162
    7.1.10 Be Patient and Confident 163
    7.1.11 The Prime Directive of Retrospectives 164
7.2 A Solution-Focused Retrospective in Five Steps 165
    7.2.1 Opening 165
    7.2.2 Set Goals 167
    7.2.3 Find Meaning 170
    7.2.4 Initiate Action 172
    7.2.5 Check Results 175
    7.2.6 A Brief, Solution-Focused Retrospective 176
Summary 177

Chapter 8   Distributed Retrospectives 179

8.1 Forms of Distributed Retrospectives 179
    8.1.1 Multiple Distributed Teams 179
    8.1.2 Teams with Singly Distributed Employees 183
    8.1.3 Scattered Teams 185
8.2 The Right Tools 186
    8.2.1 Web Whiteboard 187
    8.2.2 Stormz Hangout 188
    8.2.3 Lino 189

Contents   xiii

    8.3 General Tips for Distributed Retrospectives 190
        8.3.1 Keep It Short 190
        8.3.2 Stay within the Timeframe 190
        8.3.3 Use Stacking 190
        8.3.4 Prepare the Participants 190
        8.3.5 Use Communication Tools Effectively 191
        8.3.6 Meet Regularly 191
    Summary 191

Chapter 9   Alternative Approaches 193
    9.1 Work Retrospectives 193
        9.1.1 Set the Stage 194
        9.1.2 Gather Data 194
        9.1.3 Work Phase 195
        9.1.4 Experiences 195
    9.2 Fortune Cookie Retrospectives 196
    9.3 Powerful Questions 198
    Summary 200

Chapter 10   Typical Problems and Pitfalls 201
    10.1 Poor Preparation 201
    10.2 A Lot of Discussions but No Results 202
        10.2.1 Conflicting Opinions 202
        10.2.2 Indecision 204
        10.2.3 Lack of a Clear Time Frame 205
    10.3 Too Many Results 206
    10.4 Disinterest in (Further) Improvement 207
        10.4.1 Improvements Were Never Implemented ... 208
        10.4.2 Improvements Have No Effect 208
        10.4.3 The Team Was Not Given Enough Time 209
    10.5 Focus on the Negative 209
    10.6 Focus on Factual Topics 210
    Summary 213

Chapter 11   Change Management 215
    11.1 Agile Change Management 216
    11.2 Initiating Change Processes 217
        11.2.1 Set the Stage 217
        11.2.2 Gather Data 219

　　　　　11.2.3　Generate Insights..220
　　　　　11.2.4　Next Experiments...221
　　　　　11.2.5　Closing...223
　　　11.3　Accompanying Change Processes..............................224
　　　　　11.3.1　Set the Stage 224
　　　　　11.3.2　Check Hypotheses 224
　　　　　11.3.3　Gather Data 225
　　　　　11.3.4　Generate Insights..225
　　　　　11.3.5　Define Next Experiments 226
　　　　　11.3.6　Closing..228
　　　Summary 228

　Index..231

Reader Services

Register your copy of *Improving Agile Retrospectives* on the InformIT site for convenient access to updates and corrections as they become available. To start the registration process, go to informit.com/register and log in or create an account. Enter the product ISBN **9780134678344** and click Submit. Look on the Registered Products tab for an Access Bonus Content link next to this product, and follow that link to access any available bonus materials. If you would like to be notified of exclusive offers on new editions and updates, please check the box to receive email from us.

Please visit www.improvingagileretrospectives.com to download accompanying information to the book.

Foreword by Jutta Eckstein

I recently read the following story in a daily newspaper. In a hotel in Amman, Jordan, a businessman is waiting in front of an elevator. It is one of those big, lavish hotels, which has, in order to better meet the demands of its guests, placed six elevators next to one another. This businessman waits and waits, but the elevator doesn't come. The problem is that he is standing so close to the elevator that he fails to notice that some of the other elevators have been at his floor for a long time. Were he to take two paces backward, he would reach his goal more quickly.

This story illustrates how we humans tend to cling to an established decision or a previous experience (the elevator we have called will come and not another one). We then blindly follow the old, familiar path—"we've always done it this way" or "that's how it's always been"—instead of subjecting it to a critical assessment.

The fundamental idea of retrospectives is to pause, consider the chosen path and, in order to make better progress in the future, to correct that path by means of a (usually small) change. Actually, this approach is rooted in our DNA: the correct Latin term for the human race is not, as is commonly believed, Homo Sapiens, but Homo Sapiens Sapiens—that is, the human who thinks about thinking (or also, the human who thinks twice). It is exactly this reflection on our normal, everyday experiences that stands at the center of retrospectives.

It is often the case in projects or companies that individual team members are well aware of how things might be improved. However, it also often the case that there is insufficient time to examine the possible changes in detail. So nothing is changed, and the result is usually that the team has even less time. This situation is a vicious cycle and is aptly expressed with the old complaint: "We don't have time to sharpen the saws, we have to saw."

Retrospectives should thus also be considered part of risk management; the constant analysis of events and ensuing course corrections mean that risks can be more quickly recognized and managed. Despite the fact that retrospectives have been principally used in agile software development in order to ensure agility, the regular implementation of retrospectives can be valuable in other areas. The reason for this is partly that, as another old saying goes, you learn through mistakes. However, many companies consider making mistakes a mistake and demand instead that you "do it right the first time." But in our increasingly complex world, finding out what needs to change is not just the larger part of software development. In other areas, too, the first step is to explore which is the best path to the goal. In order to do that, you must also go down some "wrong" paths.; otherwise, you cannot know which are the right ones.

The right decisions can thus only be reached through the development of the system—and so you may well ask: why continue with this approach? Simply put, exploration is an inherent component of software development and, in today's world, many other areas.

The fostering or acceptance of a mistake-culture also demands deliberate and constant learning. Thus, through their focus on continuous development, retrospectives also contribute to the establishment of a learning organization.

Retrospectives need not only be used to find potential improvements. They also afford the opportunity to raise awareness of what already works well and what has thus far been achieved.

Team members can sometimes get to feeling that everything is going wrong, and the result is wide-spread frustration. Holding a retrospective to examine the work that is being done can help them to see that some things are actually working very well. This can increase the team's motivation.

In this book, Marc has succeeded in giving a truly comprehensive overview of retrospectives: he not only includes proven concrete methods, but also picks up on the latest developments and assesses their usefulness. Marc tackles some far from simple topics—such as divided, systemic, or solution-oriented retrospectives—and makes them practicable.

All in all, Marc has created a work that stands alone—that is, a book that offers a solid and practical foundation for those who are new to retrospectives. Furthermore, he has made sure that experienced retrospective facilitators will also find extensive inspiration and guidance in structuring retrospectives more effectively, thus contributing to continuous learning and improvement in organizations.

Enjoy using this book to forge a new path or to correct an existing one!

Jutta Eckstein

Author of *Retrospectives for Organizational Change*, *Agile Software Development with Distributed Teams*, and *Agile Software Development in the Large: Diving Into the Deep*

Preface

When I started using agile frameworks and did my first retrospective, it was love at first sight. The use of retrospectives to establish a continuous improvement process made perfect sense right from the beginning. I liked the idea of having a dedicated workshop with a clear structure that happens at regular intervals: a place and time that can be used to reflect on what happened the last weeks and months together with your teammates and a place and time to think about potential improvements based on your discoveries. And I still love to do it.

Unfortunately, still, many teams ignore the potential of this practice or start using it when it is already too late. This reminds me of one of my favorite metaphors: the lumberjack. Imagine a lumberjack in the woods cutting down trees. Over the last days and weeks, it got harder and harder to cut down the trees. It already takes hours for one tree. But he still continues doing his work, as he has promised to deliver a certain amount of wood. To still be able to deliver on time, he skips breaks, works longer in the evenings and even starts to work on Saturdays and Sundays. But all of these activities do not solve his real problem: He is getting slower and slower. If he took the time to do a retrospective, he would find out that sharpening his ax would be a good idea, or even better, buying a chainsaw. The same concept often applies to our work life. Time and again, we become so busy trying to deliver that we forget to ask whether a better way to do our jobs exists.

That's what agile retrospectives are for. Instead of getting stuck in the current, potentially suboptimal way of working, these dedicated workshops help to find new ways that might improve your situation. From my point of view, agile retrospectives are the cornerstone of a successful, continuous improvement process. Additionally, they are one of the best tools to trigger a cultural change in organizations.

They can even help in traditional change initiatives. Of course, agile retrospectives can be used in private life, too. I use them at the end of the year to do a New Year's Eve retrospective with my family.

As agile retrospectives are not regular meetings, but workshops, you must take some things into account to benefit from this technique. At the same time, you always have to cope with resistance in your organization, if you apply the results of your retrospectives. If you were part of one or more change initiatives, you know what I'm talking about. But I guess you bought this book to get some answers, right? In this book, you'll find all the ingredients you need to facilitate successful agile retrospectives and establish a continuous improvement process.

A great agile retrospective is fun, energetic, diversified, has a clear goal and purpose, and takes the system you are currently in into account. I'll walk you through the steps you must take to get there. I hope you'll find this book useful and that you enjoy reading it.

Acknowledgments

I would like to thank all the people who have directly or indirectly helped to create this book—first and foremost, all the teams for which I had the pleasure to facilitate a retrospective in the past years.

I also want to thank all the experts who reviewed earlier versions of this book and helped to turn a good book into a great book. These are (in no particular order) Srinath Ramakrishnan, Susanne Albinger, Pierre Baum, Jon Eversett, Gemma Kuijpers, Mateusz Gajdzik, Dennis Wager, and Adi Bolboaca.

A big thank you goes out to Veronika Kotrba and Ralph Miarka, who wrote the chapter about solution-focused retrospectives. It adds an additional and valuable perspective on agile retrospectives.

Another big thank you goes to Eamonn O'Leary, who translated most of the German text. It saved me a lot of time that I used to add some additional information to this book.

I'd also like to thank Lisa Crispin, who connected me with Christopher Guzikowski, my editor at Pearson. Without Lisa, you wouldn't be able to hold this book in your hands.

Special thanks to my wife Andrea, who kept my back free while writing this book. Without her, this wouldn't be possible. And of course, a big thank you to my two boys Nico and Ben, who had less time with their dad during the last month.

About the Author

Marc Loeffler is a keynote speaker, author, and agile coach. Before encountering agile methods and principles in 2006, he was working as a traditional project manager for companies like Volkswagen AG and Siemens AG. His passion is to help teams implement agile frameworks like Scrum and XP and to transform our world of work. Marc has a passion for helping teams that are struggling with agile transitions and overcoming dysfunctional behavior. He loves to generate new insights by approaching common problems from the other side and trying to wreak havoc on the process deliberately.

1

Retrospectives 101

The primary purpose of this first chapter is to introduce you to retrospectives. I'll tell you how to use retrospectives in a family context, introduce you to the phase model, and give you some hints for how to fill these phases with life. After this chapter, you will have all the basics to start with your first retrospective, so let's get started.

1.1 What Is a Retrospective?

Generally speaking, a retrospective (lat. *retrospectare*, "look back") is a review, a look backward. When you lie in bed at night and let the events of the day cross your mind, that is a retrospective. When a family sits down to dinner and talks about the day—the children talking about school and the parents talking about their experiences—that is a retrospective. Looking back over the life's work of an artist, author, or director is also a retrospective. As part of a retrospective like this, various events take place at which a range of the artist's work is shown. All the important pieces are collected in a single place to provide a complete picture of the artist's work. This makes it possible to get a good overall impression and affords the opportunity of comparing and contrasting the different works of art. This would be impossible if we had access to only one example. Only by getting the overall impression is it possible to see the whole and have the opportunity to speculate about why the artist did one thing and not another.

Another kind of retrospective takes place on television, usually at the end of every year, in the form of a year-in-review program, where the different broadcasters compete to have the funniest, most beautiful, or most famous people on their programs. Entertainment is the priority here, and there's not much emphasis on getting a full picture. These year-in-review programs are therefore rather patchy and aren't really suitable for drawing conclusions or looking at the connections between different events.

When I speak of retrospectives in this book, I mean something else. The retrospectives I discuss also involve looking back, but that is just the first step. Much more important is to gain knowledge and insight from this activity. This knowledge and insight can help us learn from the past and adapt accordingly. We can learn from both successes as well as failures; good things can often be made even better. You could compare it to evolution: things that haven't worked become extinct, but everything that contributes to the preservation of the species is kept and developed further. In the end, each of these adaptations is nothing more than an experiment, because you never know for sure what the result will be. At best, these experiments lead to an improvement of the current situation. Sometimes they do just make things worse, which we then must analyze in the next retrospective.

Every retrospective is led by a facilitator, who ensures that the group achieves the goals it sets. He helps the groups to develop practical results that will be the foundation for future success. The facilitator is not a participant (although in small teams this is not always avoidable); he accompanies the process but is not actively involved in implementing solutions. A good facilitator is essential for a successful retrospective.

This kind of retrospective was first described by Norman Kerth in his book, *Project Retrospectives: A Handbook for Team Reviews* [1]:

A retrospective is a ritual gathering of a community at the end of a project to review the events and learn from the experience. No one knows the whole story of a project. Each person has a piece of the story.

The retrospective ritual is the collective telling of the story and mining the experience for wisdom.

In his book, Kerth explains how retrospectives differ from so-called "postmortems" and "lessons learned." The main difference is that retrospectives focus on positive future actions and use them as a catalyst for change. They represent not the end of the project, but milestones in the process of continuous improvement.

In 2001, several people met in a ski lodge to write a manifesto for agile software development [2]. The foundation of the manifesto consists of four pairs of values and twelve principles. The last of these principles is an excellent description of what happens in a retrospective:

At regular intervals, the team reflects on how to become more effective, then tunes and adjusts its behavior accordingly.

This manifesto is one of the main reasons that the agile community in particular enthusiastically incorporated retrospectives into its work process. These people realized that they did not have to wait until the end of a project to learn from what had happened and make appropriate changes. Instead, they organize a retrospective after each iteration; that is, after a certain period. This interval should be no longer than one month. Otherwise, you run the risk of stretching the feedback cycle too far.

What Is an Iteration?

The word *iteration* comes from the Latin *"iterare,"* which means "repeat." Iterations are applied in a wide range of areas where problems are solved step by step. In computer science, *iteration* is the name for the process of taking different steps until the desired condition is reached (as with a FOR loop, for example). In Scrum, an iteration is called a "sprint."

I use the term *iteration* to describe the process of running a project in clearly defined, short, repetitive steps. After each iteration, you stop to determine whether and to what extent the project objective has been realized and, if necessary, adapt the original plan. The goal is to keep the risk of uncertainty and surprises to a minimum. The same procedure can also be used in change management.

Holding retrospectives enables you to establish a process of continuous improvement, which constantly checks whether or not you are on the right path and also gives you the opportunity to intervene and make any necessary changes promptly. By scheduling a dedicated time for reflection, you give yourself the opportunity to solve problems immediately, instead of having to wait until the end of the project. If you do not hold the retrospective until the end of a project, you run the risk of forgetting what you have learned before the next project. You also gain the opportunity to implement improvements in every iteration.

> **What Exactly Is the Term *"Agile"* in This Context?**
> The word agile comes from the Latin *agilis*, "to do, make, or act." As described earlier, this agility is based on the 12 principles of the Agile Manifesto [2].
>
> The Agile Manifesto is as follows: We are uncovering better ways of developing software by doing it and helping others do it. Through this work we have come to value:
>
> - Individuals and interactions over processes and tools
> - Working software over comprehensive documentation
> - Customer collaboration over contract negotiation
> - Responding to change over following a plan
>
> That is, although value exists in the items on the right, we value the items on the left more.

The corresponding 12 principles look like this:

1. Our highest priority is to satisfy the customer through early and continuous delivery of valuable software.

2. Welcome changing requirements, even late in development. Agile processes harness change for the customer's competitive advantage.

3. Deliver working software frequently, from a couple of weeks to a couple of months, with a preference to the shorter timescale.

4. Business people and developers must work together daily throughout the project.

5. Build projects around motivated individuals. Give them the environment and support they need, and trust them to get the job done.

6. The most efficient and effective method of conveying information to and within a development team is face-to-face conversation.

7. Working software is the primary measure of progress.

8. Agile processes promote sustainable development. The sponsors, developers, and users should be able to maintain a constant pace indefinitely.

9. Continuous attention to technical excellence and good design enhances agility.

10. Simplicity—the art of maximizing the amount of work not done—is essential.

11. The best architectures, requirements and designs emerge from self-organizing teams.

12. At regular intervals, the team reflects on how to become more effective, then tunes and adjusts its behavior accordingly.

As you can see, some of the principles directly target software development. However, most of the principles can also be applied easily in other areas. The agile manifesto is based on the fundamental idea that we live in a complex and unpredictable world. Therefore, creating a detailed project plan for several years or even months makes no sense. As most people who have ever planned a project know, after only a very short time, the plan bears little semblance to reality. Agile developers understand this situation and try to minimize its effect using short feedback cycles and to work closely with the customer.

Different frameworks and processes have been developed on the basis of the Agile Manifesto. Among these are XP, DSDM, Open UP, and, of course, Scrum, which is currently the most popular. At the same time, ideas from agile software development have also spread to other fields. For example, in his book *"The Leader's Guide to Radical Management"*[3], Stephen Denning describes the application of the ideas in the Agile Manifesto to the field of management.

1.2 New Year's Eve Retrospective

A few years ago, my family and I started a new Year's tradition. We call it the New Year's Eve Retrospective. Not only is it a lot of fun, but it also helps pass the time until midnight (especially helpful with children). The New Year's Eve Retrospective goes like this: To start, we all sit down together and look at some photos and watch some short videos that we took during the year. I've prepared a USB stick with the photos and videos beforehand. This phase of our retrospective is always loads of fun and results in a lot of laughter.

After this review, we have a look at our measures and hypotheses from the year. This is important because it is the only way we can determine whether or not the resolutions we made last year had the desired effect. If they didn't, we can decide whether the subject is still relevant and choose a new measure. After reviewing our hypotheses, we start to recollect all the things about the last year that have been particularly memorable. We use three categories:

- What did I like this year?
- What I did not like at all this year (or what made me angry)?
- Thank you

The first category is for all of those things that were fun or made us happy; for example, our family holiday in a kyrgyz yurt. The second category includes all the negative events. These are things like "socks everywhere" or "annoying parents." The third category simply serves to say "thank you" to your wife or mom, to the children or siblings, and so on. Connecting your gratitude to a specific case is always important. For example, "Thanks for letting me play with your Skylander toys" or "Thank you for making me a snack every morning."

'It is then time to gain knowledge and insights. Each family member is allowed to choose a topic that he or she finds particularly important, and these topics are discussed in turn. The goal of these discussions is to find the underlying causes for the topic. At the moment, we're finding the 5-Why question method very valuable here

> **5-Why Method**
> This method starts with the question: "why is x happening?" or "why does x always happen?" The answer serves as the basis for the next "why" question. You then repeat the process, digging deeper and deeper until, hopefully, you've found the real cause. We make sure to write this cause on a piece of paper because it is the foundation of the next phase. The 5-Why method is around 100 years old and was created by Sakichi Toyota [5], the founder of Toyota, to get to the bottom of production problems and so prevent them from re-occurring.

The next step is to use the causes we've found to create concrete, measurable resolutions for next year. To this end, we have a short brainstorming session to collect ideas about our topics. You wouldn't believe the ideas children can come up with, even for the topics closer to their parents' hearts. Everyone presents his or her ideas for each topic, and we choose the most promising idea. We make our choice by sticking colored dots up next to the ideas on the paper. This technique is called "Dot Voting." Each of us has three sticky dots, which we can put wherever we like. Once we've finished, we place the newly chosen measures in a prominent place: our family corkboard in the hall, which is our highly visual to-do list. There is nothing worse than results that are not visible after the retrospective. Our board helps us to keep an eye on our new measures and ensure that we actually implement them. Importantly, we also link each measure to a testable hypothesis that we can review in the next retrospective.

Of course, a retrospective also needs a worthy ending. 'In this case, the choice is easy: the New Year's Eve fireworks.

1.3 The Retrospective Phase Model

If you were paying close attention in the preceding section, you might have noticed that we went through six phases during the New Year's Eve retrospective, as illustrated in Figure 1-1.

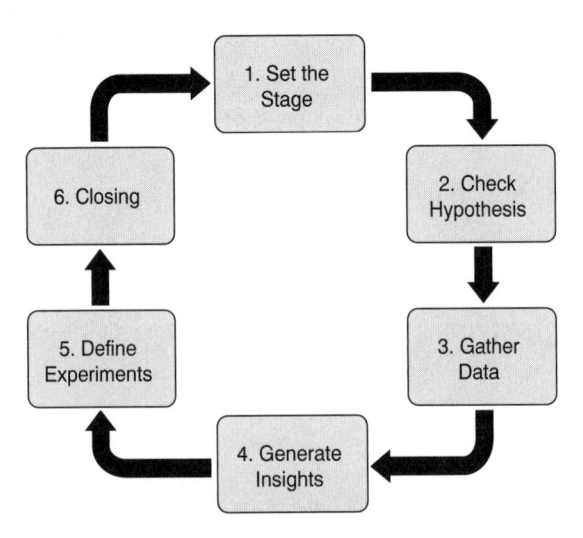

Figure 1-1 The six phases of a retrospective

These form the structure of a retrospective and are based on the original phase model in Esther Derby and Diana Larsen's book [5]. The model I describe here is an expanded form of Derby and Larsen's, the big differences being that I introduced the "Check Hypothesis" step and extended the "Define Experiments" step to include hypotheses. I explain the reasons for this later in the book. In the following sections, I explain the six phases in more detail.

1.3.1 Phase 1: Set the Stage

The first phase of a retrospective should set the stage. This phase is very important because every participant has to be mentally "picked up" from somewhere else. If you leave out this phase, you run the risk of one or more participants being mentally absent from the retrospective as they are still thinking about the last piece of work they were doing before walking in. Preparing the ground serves to get all the participants' attention and get them involved. Starting with a few words of welcome and thanking everyone for taking part is best. Then you as a facilitator briefly explain the reason for and the aim of the retrospective as well as the timeframe and the agenda. The agenda is important because, after all, we all want to know what we're spending our time on.

> **Practical Tip**
>
> Make sure that everyone in the room says something (brief). Someone who is silent at this stage is likely to remain so for the rest of the retrospective. However, it is very important that every voice be heard, because only then you will be able to get a complete picture. The participants don't all have to tell long stories; a few words per person is enough. For example, you might have people say their name or describe their expectations of the retrospective in a single word. Interestingly, this simple technique works so well in most cases that the quieter and silent team members will also participate in the discussions.

The last step of the first phase is also very important. The aim is to create an atmosphere in which difficult topics can be addressed. Only in an atmosphere where even unpleasant things can be discussed is it possible to get to the bottom of things and to address the real causes of problems. Moreover, that is the basis for a successful retrospective. What happens in Vegas, stays in Vegas.

You create this atmosphere by establishing the rules for cooperation, or the "working agreement." Some teams have already defined the values they have for their daily work, and in that case, you should use those values and simply remind the team of them. You might need to adjust a few values to the retrospective. The same applies, of course, if the team has already defined rules for collaboration. Many agile teams create a team charter at the beginning of their collaboration.

> **What Is a Team Charter?**
> A team charter defines all the rules for teamwork, including the rules for communication and conduct as well as the timing and length of regular meetings. Software development teams also have a list of the development tools they use and possibly links to further information. The team charter is, among other things, a good starting point for new team members. It should be a living document that is iteratively developed. If any team member feels and expresses that the charter should be adjusted, then the team discusses that request and, upon agreement, adjusts.

If there are no rules for cooperation yet, now is the time to define them. However, why are these rules so important? The following is a brief example.

Let's say your colleague James has the habit of taking his laptop with him into every meeting. He uses the time in these meetings to answer his e-mails or surf the web. If you start the retrospective without clearly pre-established rules, he will probably do that same thing. It will annoy everyone, but no one will have the rules to point to and ask him to close the laptop. However, if the rules have been defined in advance, they can be pointed out at any time. Another advantage of having common rules for cooperation is that all the participants are responsible for observing them. This makes it easier for the facilitator to concentrate on the actual work of the retrospective.

> **Practical Tip**
>
> If the team does not yet have a team charter, invite members to a workshop immediately after the retrospective in order to create one.

Unfortunately, this is the phase of the retrospective that is most frequently skipped because people want to save time and get started right away. In my experience, taking a team through this phase has never been a waste of time. If the team has been working together for a long time, it often takes no more than five minutes. Five minutes

- that minimize the risk of someone not speaking
- that make sure that everyone feels they are in a safe environment in which to work
- to get everyone present and let them clear their heads for this important meeting

Sometimes it can also be five minutes of fun. For example, you might ask the team: "If the last iteration were a car, what kind of car would it be?" All it takes is one or two words, and you get everybody mentally present.

> **Check-In**
>
> This check-in technique is described in Derby and Larsen's book [5, p. 42] and is implemented after you have welcomed the participants and presented the goal of the retrospective. The facilitator asks a short question, which each participant answers in turn as quickly as possible. Here are a few example questions:
>
> - In one or two words, what do you hope for from this retrospective?
> - If the last iteration were a country, which country would it be?
> - What kind of weather word (sunny, cloudy, rainy, thunderstorm) would you use to describe your present mood?
>
> It is okay for a participant to say "pass." Even that one word is enough for his voice to be heard.

As a reminder, in our New Year's Eve retrospective, we set the stage by looking at the photos and videos from the past year. Believe me—it's a lot of fun!

1.3.2 Phase 2: Check Hypothesis

The purpose of the Check Hypothesis phase is to review the hypotheses created at the last retrospective. Ideally, these hypotheses are created from the experiments chosen (see section 1.3.5). However, why is this step so important?

Let's say that during the last retrospective you discussed the problem of very poor communication with the product management team. The product manager is hard to reach, and questions are only answered after major delays. At the end of the last retrospective, you decided on a measure to be taken: The product manager would now be available to the team for a specific time slot every day. This time would be for discussing current questions and getting answers, thus reducing delays to a minimum. The hypothesis that you connected to this experiment might have been as follows: "Current questions will now be answered in less than 24 hours." This would be a real improvement on the recent situation, in which the team sometimes had to wait several weeks for a response.

After the stage has been set, the team checks the hypotheses. It turns out that the experiment was wrong. It seems that although the response time is getting a little better, it is still far from the 24-hour mark. So, the problem remains. In the further course of this retrospective, the team will, therefore, try to pinpoint the causes of this problem and then either adapt the current experiment or define a new one. During this process, it might discover, for example, that the product manager was never consulted about the new change and was simply told to implement it. Rather than motivating him to work more closely with the team, this just made him angry. Using hypotheses enables the team to work on a topic until the problem is either solved or reduced to a tolerable level.

> **Practical Tip**
>
> If any of your hypotheses are not confirmed as you expected, use the next phases of the retrospective to find out why.

This example shows that hypotheses are an important tool. Some teams merely check whether or not the measures chosen in the previous retrospective were actually implemented. Only a few bother to check whether those measures also had the desired effect. However, only by checking for the desired effect can you actually create improvement. This is certainly not a panacea, but it is effective in most cases. Hypotheses also help to make retrospectives meaningful and help you to stay focused on a topic instead of letting the discussion wander.

1.3.3 Phase 3: Gather Data

Now we come to the actual looking back invoked in the word *"retrospective."* The aim of the Gather Data phase is to collect data on a clearly defined period from the past. This could be the last iteration (or sprint in Scrum), the period of an entire project, or even the last working day. The time between an event considered and the retrospective should be kept as short as possible. Your main goal in this phase is to create a common understanding of the period you are considering. Without this common picture, the participants might not understand one another's perspectives and opinions and will tend to project their feelings onto others. To create a common picture, everyone gets the opportunity to present his or her view of things.

You start by collecting the hard facts. These facts can be anything that took place during this period, from meetings and decisions to personal experiences. Include everything that had and has a meaning for anybody on the team here. Numbers (measures) might also feature in this step; for example, the number of completed requirements, or the number of closed, open, and new errors. The more memorable the result, the better.

You could simply talk about all of these things, but including a visualization is much better. A visualization simplifies the recording of information and is indispensable, especially in the case of longer retrospectives. One example of a visualization is a timeline laid out on a wall, which allows you to see the temporal relationships between events (see Figure 1-2).

Figure 1-2 Gather data using a timeline

Although the hard facts are important, they are still only part of the story. Just as important are the personal perspectives that people have on the time being considered because these tell us which events are more important and which are less so. Collecting both facts and personal perspectives helps to focus on the issues that have most affected the team. At the same time, the emotional quality of these perspectives also reveals the situations in which people felt good. Knowing when people felt good gives you the opportunity to re-create this situation more often. A further reason to discuss emotional issues is that, though they have the potential to become a drain on energy and motivation in daily working life, they are often overlooked.

Only by talking to your team can you find out what is going on and put yourself in a position to address concerns, eliminate negatives, and strengthen positives.

> **Definition of the Term "*Team*"**
> When I use the term *team* in this book, I'm talking about any form of team in the professional context. This could be a software development team, a team of HR people, or any other kind of team. It could even be the team of your sport club. In other words, a team is a group of people working together to achieve a common goal.

Before moving on to the next step, take the time with the team to get an overall picture of the period you are reviewing. You can do this by having each team member present his or her insights, or by giving the whole team some time to reflect on the information you have collected (using the timeline, for example).

Reminder: In the New Year's retrospective, we collected the data by *sorting* events into three categories:

- What did I like this year?
- What did I not like at all this year (or what made me angry)?
- Thank you

Each of us then briefly presents the topic we've chosen. By using emotional words in the question, we set ourselves up to get a combination of hard facts and feelings. Experience has shown me that this phase of the retrospective should be varied very often. I will talk about possible variations in the chapters throughout this book. If you can't wait, have a look at the later section 1.4.

1.3.4 Phase 4: Generate Insights

You use the Generate Insights phase to understand the context of the situation as well as possible causes and connections. You analyze the events collected in the previous phase and then ask, "Why did these things happen?" What you are looking for are insights into the fundamental causes of the events that took place.

After the first phase, this phase is the next most frequently omitted. Many teams skip this phase and immediately try to define future experiments without considering the possible causes of the current situation. This means that they only ever scratch the surface and that their measures will only treat the symptoms instead of dealing with the root causes. It's like using pain killers, when you actually broke your leg. The pain will vanish for a short period of time, but because the root cause wasn't addressed, the pain will come back. This is not a good idea because what might seem a promising path out of your problem often leads you straight back into it. On the other hand, carrying this phase out well provides you with a solid foundation for the next phase: define experiments and their hypotheses. Do not try to tackle all of your problems at once. Instead, choose the issues that the group feels are the most important. You won't be able to solve all of your problems in a single retrospective. This phase is designed to help the team step back, see the whole picture, and start looking for the root causes. It doesn't make sense to work on more than three topics during the next iteration, as these topics won't be the only thing you have to work on, right? You need the insights gained in this phase to define reasonable and effective measures.

Remember, during our New Year's Eve retrospective, every family member is allowed to choose the topic that is most important to him or her and which he or she would like to discuss at this stage. We currently use the "5 Whys" to look for causes. When our children get older, we will vary the technique we use.

1.3.5 Phase 5: Define Experiments

The first four phases have set up a strong foundation for the Define Experiments phase. You've created an overall picture and common understanding of the period under consideration and have also gained some insight into the various events that took place. At this point, most of the team will already have some ideas about what to improve or try out next. So the team's next task is to choose one or two actions and to agree on how to implement them. This also ensures that the team will have the time to implement its decisions. After all, the daily workload still must be done. Trying to implement too many changes at once can lead to problems. It also makes it more difficult to tell later which experiments actually had an effect.

I use the word *'experiments'* deliberately here. Nobody knows what will happen if you try something out. Although we may have an idea of what might happen (our hypothesis), no one can actually be sure. An analogy for this is a lab researcher who creates an experiment to test his hypothesis. Only at the end of the experiment will he be able to tell whether or not it actually worked. The most effective way to work with these experiments is to repeat your retrospectives at regular intervals that are as short as possible. This creates a safe space: An experiment that is going wrong will make less mess if you cut it off quickly rather than let it run rampant.

Just as important as the definition of the experiment itself is the definition of the corresponding *hypothesis*. You carry out experiments not (just) for fun, but because you think it will create an effect.

The hypothesis allows you to determine the extent of an experiment's effect in the next retrospective. So, hypotheses must be testable. A hypothesis such as, "This will lead to fewer errors in the software" is vague and harder to assess meaningfully. A better version of this hypothesis is, "The number of known errors in the software will be reduced to ten or less." You must always consider how your hypothesis is to be tested. This is the only way to make hypotheses meaningful and to use them to define new experiments if the first proves unsuccessful.

> **Practical Tip**
> Explicitly explain to the team that any action defined in this phase is nothing more than an experiment. No one can be certain beforehand of what the actual outcome will be.

Making the results of the retrospective visible to everyone is good practice. Agile teams, like a Scrum team, always include the defined experiments in the next planning session. The experiments chosen are considered part of the normal workload and are not extra tasks. That's exactly how it should be. It is also important that the team is willing to carry out these tasks. Having a single person take responsibility for each experiment is best. This person does not have to carry out the experiment alone but is responsible for ensuring that action is taken. If nobody is assigned responsibility now, you're likely to find that no one feels responsible for carrying out the experiment.

We used sticky dots (like those shown in Figure 1-3) to choose the experiments during the New Year's Eve retrospective. We then displayed these experiments on our corkboard to keep their status in mind. There's nothing worse than task lists that get lost in some document, wiki, or email.

CHAPTER 1 • RETROSPECTIVES 101   **19**

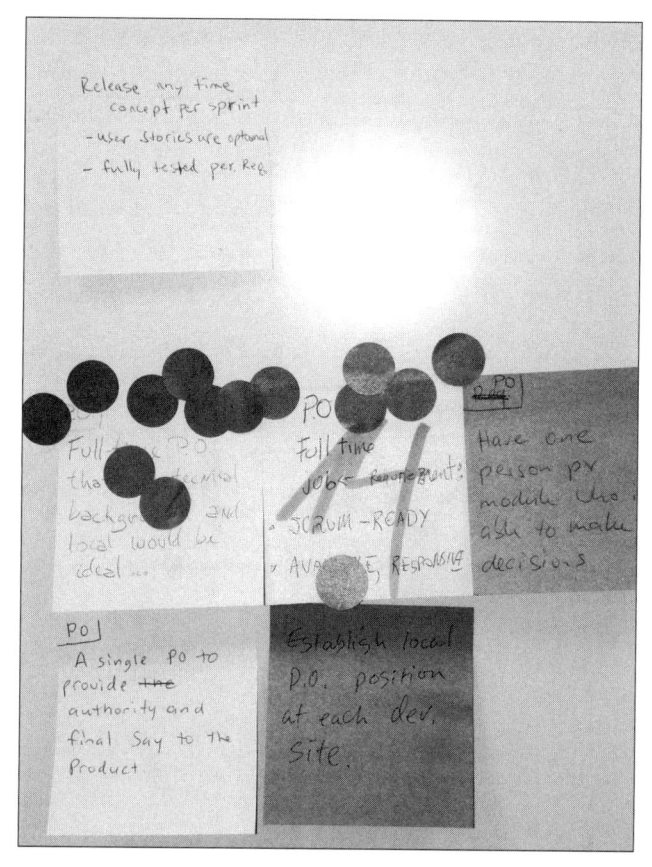

Figure 1-3 Dot voting

1.3.6 Phase 6: Closing

To conclude, spend a few minutes on a short review and celebrate the results of your retrospective. This honors the time and energy that the team has put into both the retrospective and the preceding time span or iteration. You should also document your results appropriately. There are many ways to do this, including taking photographs of the whiteboard and keeping the flipchart paper the team used to

20 IMPROVING AGILE RETROSPECTIVES

develop their ideas. As described earlier, display these things very visibly in the team's workroom. Finally, the facilitator summarizes on how to proceed. This is to check that everyone understands the plan.

As a very last step, having a brief retrospective on the retrospective itself is always a good idea. After all, you want continuous improvement to extend to your retrospectives, too. One tool for this is a ROTI (Return on Time Invested) graph, as shown in Figure 1-4.

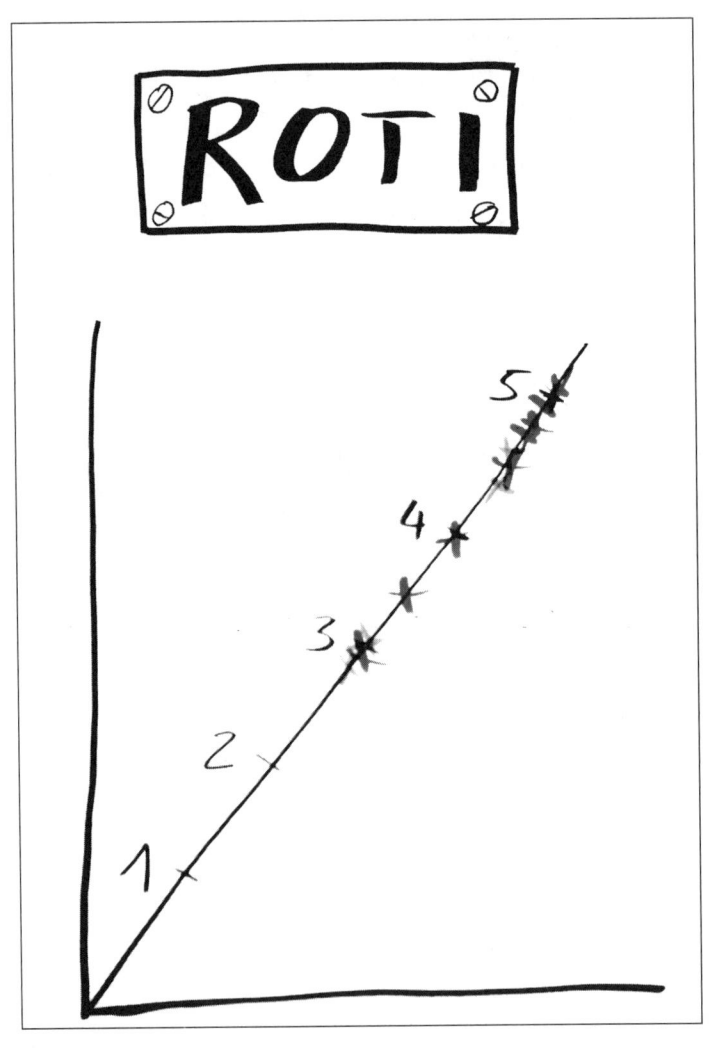

Figure 1-4 ROTI (Return on Time Invested)

What Is a Return on Time Invested (ROTI) Graph?

A ROTI graph is often used after a meeting to get some quick feedback from a team. It is a good way to determine whether your retrospectives are working well or whether they need to be improved. To create a ROTI graph, simply draw x and y axes and then a diagonal line numbered from one to five. One means, "This meeting was a total waste of time." Three means, "This meeting was just about worth the time I invested in attending." Five means, "This meeting was absolutely fantastic; the time I invested in attending paid off incredibly well." Each participant adds a cross to the graph to show his or her opinion, and the result is the completed graph. As you can see in Figure 1-4, this team was quite happy with their retrospective.

My family and I were able to celebrate our New Year's Eve retrospective with a beautiful fireworks display. Unfortunately, you can't do this every day, but a delicious slice of cake at the end of a retrospective can also provide a great ending.

Practical Tip

The time you'll need to spend on each phase of a retrospective depends, of course, on the activities you select for each phase, as well as on the total amount of time at your disposal. In general, however, the time you'll spend on each phase can be reliably calculated as a percentage of the total time. By way of example, here are the phase timings for a 60-minute retrospective:

1. Set the stage (5 minutes = 1/12 time)
2. Check hypotheses (5 minutes = 1/12 time)
3. Gather data (10 minutes = 1/6 time)
4. Generate insights (20 minutes = 1/3 of the time)

> 5. Define experiments (15 minutes = 1/4 time)
> 6. Conclusion (5 minutes = 1/12 time)
>
> These timings are only a general rule, but they are a reliable place to start when planning your retrospectives.

The phase model provides you with a simple framework that will help you to plan and carry out retrospectives effectively. Keep to this framework, and you'll have an ideal foundation. Remember, though, that each and every retrospective is unique. These six phases have been tested many times, and they work. In the rest of the book, you will learn how to bring this model to life as well as how to deal with the typical difficulties that can arise.

1.4 Finding Activities for Each of the Phases

The six phases are just a framework which helps you to structure retrospectives. Like many frameworks, it tells you what to do, but does not specify how. Your task then, is to bring these phases to life and you do that by finding a range of activities to carry out in each of the phases. The activities you choose should be appropriate to the goal of each phase and, when you're still new to retrospectives, it to finding something suitable can be difficult.

> **Practical Tip**
> As you're starting out, avoid the temptation to find a new activity for each phase every time you do a retrospective. Just try out a few activities at first.

Many experienced retrospective facilitators have written about their ideas and made them available in books and on the Internet. In the following sections, I present some of the sources I have used.

Later in the book, you will also learn a few techniques for generating your own activities, but the following sources are an excellent place to start.

> **Practical Tip**
>
> When choosing activities, make sure that they dovetail. You need to be able to use the results you get from an activity in one phase in the following phase. You can't choose activities at random. Just as you'll only be able to cook a good meal if your ingredients work well together, you'll only have an effective retrospective if your activities work well together.

1.4.1 Agile Retrospectives Book

"Agile Retrospectives: Making Good Teams Great" by Esther Derby and Diana Larsen [5] was the first book to discuss retrospectives in the context of agile software development and is one of the key texts on retrospectives in general. After a brief introduction to the topic and the description of the phase model, the writers swiftly move on to the practical component. Eighty percent of the book consists of descriptions of activities that can be carried out in the different phases. The description of each activity includes the goal, the time required, the individual steps, the materials required, and possible variations.

Derby and Larsen describe a total of 38 activities, which provides enough material for quite a few retrospectives. Combining these activities in different ways means you can keep a sense of variety and novelty in your retrospectives over a long period.

1.4.2 Retromat

I came across the Retromat [6] website by chance and have recommended it as often as possible ever since. No other source enables you to find activities for your retrospectives as easily as it does. It was created by Corinna Baldauf [7].

The first time you visit the site, you immediately get a suggested retrospective plan with different activities proposed for each phase. If you don't like those activities, you can either generate a completely new plan, or click through different activities per phase until you find what you want. The activities on the site come from various sources, including Derby and Larsen's book. Each plan has a reference number that allows you to find it again or share it with other people. As of the writing of this book, Retromat offers 131 activities, and more are always being added. Retromat also allows you to enter your own activities.

1.4.3 Retrospective Wiki

Another great source for ideas on designing your retrospective is the Retrospective Wiki [8], which contains a list of possible activities and complete plans. This wiki also features some tips and tricks, descriptions of typical problems and potential solutions, and links to further sources. Many of the activities included will be familiar from the other sources I've described, but you will also find some new ideas. This wiki is constantly expanded and maintained.

1.4.4 Tasty Cupcakes

Tasty Cupcakes isn't really dedicated to retrospectives but features a wide range of games and simulations that can be used in all areas of life. For example, you might find a workshop on product innovation or a simulation to make it easier to understand a particular topic. This website was created by Michael McCullough and Don McGreal after they presented a variety of games at the Agile2008 conference. They were assisted by Michael Sahota.

Several of the ideas on the site can be used in retrospectives. Just click on the words "retrospective" or "retrospectives" in the tag cloud' to get a list of possible activities. This site is constantly being expanded and maintained, so 'having a look from time to time is worthwhile [9].

1.4.5 Gamestorming

Gamestorming [10] is a wonderful collection of creative games that support innovation and implementing change. Some people might be put off by the word *'game,'* but the creative techniques presented in the book are more like playful approaches to work than games.

This book is a practical reference with a total of 88 different activities, most of which can be used very easily in retrospectives. After all, a retrospective is nothing if not a catalyst for change. The activities are divided into four categories:

- Core Games
- Games for Opening
- Games for Exploring
- Games for Closing

The names of these categories have some overlap with the six phases of a retrospective. "Games for Opening," for example, are likely to work well in the "Set the Stage" phase. The activities listed under "Games for Exploring" are suited to both the "Gather Data" as well as "Generate Insights" phases. "Games for Closing" can be used in "Define Experiments" and to conclude the retrospective.

Here is a possible plan for a retrospective using activities from *"Gamestorming"*:

- Set the Stage: Draw the Problem (p. 90)
- Gather Data: Pain-Gain Map (p. 190)
- Generate Insights: Understanding Chain (p. 218)
- Define Experiments: Prune the Future (p. 247)
- Closing: Plus/Delta (p. 246)

The book provides key information for each activity, including the goal, a detailed description of the process, and an approximate runtime, which helps with planning. Also included is a piece of information that is important if you want to carry out the activity effectively: the number of participants.

In addition to the activities, the book features a good introduction to the idea of game storming as well as provides you with the information you need to start creating your own activities. This book is a must for anyone serious about retrospectives and implementing change.

1.5 The Prime Directive

Some facilitators begin their retrospectives by reading out the fundamental principle, the Prime Directive. First articulated by Norman Kerth in his book, *Project Retrospectives: A Handbook for Team Reviews* [1], the Prime Directive is designed to set the stage for the retrospective:

Regardless of what we discover, we understand and truly believe that everyone did the best job they could, given what they knew at the time, their skills and abilities, the resources available, and the situation at hand.

This principle is read aloud at the beginning of a retrospective, precisely in this wording.

The idea is to make it clear to everyone that we are all human and make mistakes. The principle also points out that we shouldn't assume that things have been done badly deliberately.

> **Practical Tip**
> You don't need to read out the Prime Directive at every retrospective. In later retrospectives, simply reminding people of it is enough.

Many retrospective facilitators swear by the Prime Directive. They feel that retrospectives that don't start with this fundamental principle are less effective and therefore less useful. Pat Kua writes

[Kua 2012] that this is related to the *Pygmalion* [11] or *Rosenthal* effect, or what is commonly known as "'a self-fulfilling prophecy.'"

The effect of a teacher's preconceptions about his students might be an example of the Rosenthal effect. The idea is that a teacher's positive preconception about a student ('that student is a high achiever') will affect the teacher's behavior in such a way as to create confirmation of his expectations. What happens is that the teacher subtly transmits his preconception to the student through, for example, more one-to-one attention, more time given for response, frequency and strength of praise or blame, or high-performance requirements. This is an unconscious rather than deliberate course of action.

In essence, the theory is that someone who is treated as having certain characteristics will manifest them. In fact, Rosenthal's results were repeatedly called into question and could only be reproduced in 40 percent of cases [11].

I personally believe that the success of a retrospective depends not on the careful reading out of the Prime Directive, but rather upon the values that it describes. I have carried out many successful retrospectives during which I did not explicitly mention the Prime Directive. I'm not saying that reading the principle isn't a good thing; in new teams or established teams that are about to experience their first retrospective, this ritual can have a very positive, if not measurable, effect. In my experience, however, you lose that positive effect if you read out the directive at every retrospective. Repetition does to the directive what frequent flying does to pre-flight safety briefings. The first time you fly, you pay close attention. However, with prolonged exposure, you pay less and less attention until, in the end, you hardly notice it's happening.

A positive attitude is essential for a successful retrospective, but I believe there are many ways to achieve that attitude and the Prime Directive is only one (and one that is certainly no guarantee of success).

There is also an alternative prime directive that is somewhat longer but may work better for some teams [12]. I personally like the fact that it is written in the first person and is thus more appealing:

Some days are better than others. Some days I'm in the "flow" state, doing awesome work. Some days I come to the end of a day and realized I've wasted a lot of time, made mistakes that I should have foreseen, or wish I could have done something differently.

Regardless, those days have happened and our purpose here is to find out:

What can we learn from our past actions and thinking that will inform and guide our future actions and thinking so that we can do a little better?

How can we change our environment ("the system") so that it's easier for us to do awesome work and less likely for us for us to waste time and make mistakes?

Like the original Prime Directive, this version describes the goal of a retrospective and articulates the underlying principles. Also like the original, this alternative is just a tool and does not guarantee a successful retrospective. My advice is that you experiment with both versions and see what kind of an impact it has on your retrospectives. When properly used, the Prime Directive can be a valuable tool.

Summary

In this book, I describe what retrospectives are and how to use them to establish a process of continuous improvement. Looking back into the past is only a part of a retrospective, and not even the most important. Retrospectives should be used to help you gain insights and try new things, to create and carry out experiments and to question them, too. That is the best way to support a goal-oriented and meaningful process of continuous improvement and constant learning.

Although retrospectives are still most commonly used in working life, as at the end of projects or in the form of "heartbeat" retrospectives in agile teams, they can be usefully applied to any area of life, as in our New Year's Eve retrospective.

A six-phase process that defines the framework for retrospectives will help you to make retrospectives as effective as possible:

- Set the Stage
- Check Hypotheses
- Gather Data
- Generate Insights
- Define Experiments
- Closing

Each phase can be brought to life with a range of activities, which, when regularly changed, will bring fresh energy and ideas into the process. You can either design these activities yourself or turn to one of the many books or websites available.

Starting retrospectives by reading out the Prime Directive can help to prepare the ground for a successful retrospective, but you should remember that doing so does not guarantee a successful outcome.

Ultimately, the success of a retrospective lies with the facilitator and the participating team. In the chapters that follow, I describe the keys to success and the common pitfalls to avoid.

References

[1] Norman Kerth. 2001. *Project Retrospectives: A Handbook for Team Reviews.* New York: Dorset House Publishing Co Inc.

[2] Manifesto for Agile Software Development. http://agilemanifesto.org.

[3] Steve Denning. 2010. *The Leader's Guide to Radical Management: Reinventing the Workplace for the 21st Century.* San Francisco, CA: Jossey-Bass.

[4] Sakichi Toyoda. https://en.wikipedia.org/wiki/Sakichi_Toyoda.

[5] Esther Derby and Diana Larsen. 2006. *Agile Retrospectives: Making Good Teams Great.* Farnham, Surrey UK/: O'Reilly Ltd.

[6] Retromat. https://plans-for-retrospectives.com.

[7] Website of Corinna Baldauf. http://finding-marbles.com/

[8] Retrospective Wiki. http://retrospectivewiki.org.

[9] Tasty Cupcakes. http://tastycupcakes.org/

[10] Gray et al. 2010. *Gamestorming: A Playbook for Innovators, Rulebreakers, and Changemakers.* Sebastopol, CA: O'Reilly.

[11] Pygmalion Effect. https://en.wikipedia.org/wiki/Pygmalion_effect.

[12] Ted M. Young. *The Alternative Prime Directive.* http://jitterted.com/2013/02/11/another-alternative-to-the-retrospective-prime-directive/

2

Preparing Retrospectives

Before we can finally start to facilitate our first retrospective, we need to prepare a few things, such as who should take part, prepare the room, or make sure that the right material is available. In this chapter, I'll go through all the necessary steps to do so. Never underestimate the value of investing in proper preparation. It helps you to run the whole event more smoothly. As Alexander Graham Bell said, "Before anything else, preparation is the key to success."

2.1 Preparation

You must answer a few questions before you plan your retrospective. It only makes sense to get into details after you have a clear picture of what you want the retrospective to be. Preparation will differ from retrospective to retrospective. Logically, the amount of time you need for preparation depends on the length of the retrospective.

In an emergency, an experienced facilitator can conjure up a retrospective in a few minutes. Most facilitators are not magicians, and this method should be the exception. Try it only after you've had some practice leading retrospectives.

2.1.1 What Period of Time Should Be Discussed?

You must clarify what period of time you will be considering in the retrospective. For a retrospective dealing with a whole project, a longer period is usually preferable. In my experience, however, looking back more than twelve months makes little sense. This is because after that length of time, people's memories are no longer fresh and their inability to remember many details often leads to a distortion of the facts.

In the case of *heartbeat* retrospectives, the periods considered are usually quite short (maximum four weeks). These retrospectives are performed at regular intervals (every two weeks, for example). The advantage here is that participants can still remember the events very well and, because the project is still on-going, they have the opportunity to react to problems early on. Another benefit to this approach is that you can try new things with relatively little risk because you can check what effect the experiment had during the next retrospective.

> **Practical Tip**
> Documenting all the steps of a retrospective and keeping some kind of checklist are especially helpful as you start out, to ensure you don't forget anything.

2.1.2 Who Should Take Part?

Determining who should take part is an important question because the participants have the greatest influence on a retrospective. Every single member of the team brings his or her own visions and behaviors and thus influences the retrospective. Knowing the participants gives you an advantage. For example, knowing who likes to be the center of attention and talk a lot and who the more introverted team members are enables you to plan accordingly.

In principle, the best practice is to have everyone involved in the project in any way participate in the retrospective. This makes it possible to address problems that extend beyond the core team. The participation of executives such as the head of the department can have an immense effect, especially if he is known as a dominant or controlling person. In this case, one effect is that many ideas and opinions may not be expressed openly. However, the presence of executives can have a positive effect, such as when they are able to approve decisions on the spot, approve funds, or declare themselves willing to take ideas to upper management. However, in most cases, focusing on the main team and only inviting executives if needed is a good idea.

> **Practical Tip**
>
> The team itself should always make the decision whether to have people from outside the team participate. Please contact the team before sending out invitations.

Last but not least, the number of participants is a fundamental factor. This determines the choice of venue and the number of facilitators necessary. It also plays a role in choosing activities for each phase; not all activities can be carried out with large groups.

2.1.3 Is There a Topic?

Not all retrospectives have a declared topic. In heartbeat retrospectives, for example, the important topics will come up naturally.

However, in some retrospectives, having a declared topic is useful. This is particularly true of retrospectives carried out at the end of a project or retrospectives being used to tackle specific problems.

Possible topics include conflicts in the team or projects that have gone completely off course. Having a topic also makes sense if the retrospective is intended to generate ideas on how to get yourself out of a confused situation.

> **Practical Tip**
>
> If you do have a topic for a retrospective, you need to announce it in the invitation. You should present it at the beginning in the "Set the stage" phase.

2.2 The Right Time, the Right Place

When is the right time for a retrospective? It depends on what process a team is working with. In an agile team, a retrospective takes place at the end of every iteration.

> **Practical Tip**
> In the case of regular retrospectives, make sure they are always held on the same day of the week and at the same time. This helps the team to find and maintain a rhythm, as they know exactly when the retrospectives take place and can plan accordingly. This creates a good atmosphere.

All other kinds of retrospectives are tied to a particular event, usually the end of a project. This could be a project in working life, like the launch of a product, or a project in social life, like a club anniversary or an orchestra's annual concert. It might also be a personal retrospective on your birthday. All of these events are ideal moments for reflection and further development.

After you know when you want to hold a retrospective, you have to find the right place for it. An ideal room for retrospectives meets the following criteria:

- It is large enough for all the participants—the bigger, the better.
- It has enough wall space available for hanging up flipchart paper and sticky notes.
- The tables and chairs can be easily moved to form a circle.
- The room is bright; daylight is best.
- All the technological requirements are available (whiteboard, flipchart, and possibly a projector).
- Does the room offer the freedom to speak and discuss without bothering others?

You should make it a habit of going into the room thirty to sixty minutes before the start of your retrospective to get everything set up. This is time well spent, especially for half- or full-day retrospectives. Here is a brief checklist you can use:

- Is the agenda up and clearly visible throughout the room?
- Does each participant have a pen and sticky notes?
- Is the Prime Directive (if you're using it) clearly visible throughout the room?
- Does your technology all work?
- Do you have enough flipchart paper?
- Do the pens for the whiteboard and flipchart work?
- Is there enough space available for the activities you've chosen?
- Are all the activities you've chosen practicable?
- Is there something for the participants to eat and drink?

This list will get you well set up for the retrospective. Having some of the things on the list in your personal toolbox (pens, for example) is always best so as to avoid embarrassment and wasting your participant's time if anything is missing.

Practical Tip

Changing rooms regularly, especially for heartbeat retrospectives, is a good idea. This variety can help release new energies. If you can, getting out of the office is also a good idea. Why not hold your retrospective in some nearby woods or on the banks of a lake or river? This change of venue can open up the possibility of letting the surrounding environment influence the retrospective.

You might ask, for example, what makes the team different from this big, living tree and what you can learn from it? Or you could go around the corner to your favorite Italian place and have retrospective there. Even if you can't leave the premises, changing rooms will have a big impact.

2.3 The Right Material

You might be a good craftsman, but if you don't have the right tools, you can't expect the best results. If the only tool I have to fell a tree is a jigsaw, then I'll manage it somehow, but I'm certainly not going to be particularly effective. The same is true of retrospectives. Without the right materials, retrospectives can quickly become frustrating experiences. Having sticky notes start dropping off the wall halfway through a retrospective can be extremely annoying, as can having your markers give up the ghost.

When choosing the right materials, either see the room beforehand, or at least find out what facilities are available. You can have the world's best note cards to pin up, but without a corkboard, they'll be completely useless. Knowing what a room has to offer allows you to prepare properly.

2.3.1 The Right Markers

Markers are important. Markers that won't write, or barely do so, are more than annoying. You're at the whiteboard or the flipchart, ready to get something down and just at that moment, the marker goes dry. The best thing to do in this situation is to throw the thing straight into the trashcan. If it's a refillable marker, put it to one side to be replenished at the next opportunity. This will stop you from throwing it back into your toolbox and wasting a few minutes later today or at the next meeting.

As a facilitator, bring your own markers. This ensures that you have good-quality markers with enough ink in them. My favorites are wedge-tipped markers in different sizes and colors. Wedge tips are best because you can use them to draw both thin and thick lines, which gives you more creative options. I also recommend high-quality, refillable markers.

> **Practical Tip**
>
> Test your markers before the retrospective. This ensures that you don't get any nasty surprises during the retrospective and that you have enough time to get any replacements you need. Always add a set of reserve markers to your facilitator's bag.

As the facilitator, your job is to help the team get its work done, and because this is often group work, the participants also need writing material. You don't have to be quite as choosy with these. Felt-tip pens are a good choice, but most other pens will work. The only exception is when you are working with self-adhesive film or electrostatic writing sheets. You need waterproof markers for these because standard markers make the films difficult to write on (the solvent used is too intense). Markers for use with overheads or highlighters with thick tips are the better choices.

2.3.2 The Right Sticky notes

There are sticky notes, and then there are sticky notes. Most widely available sticky notes are not suitable for retrospectives. They might just stick to your monitor, but they don't usually work on a wall or whiteboard.

If you want sticky notes that will work, you should spend a bit more money on ones with a stronger adhesive. Super Stickies are more adhesive than normal sticky notes. They'll stick to normal walls and even concrete. You can be sure they won't come tumbling off the wall.

If you're not interested in sticky notes, there's still the variant I mentioned above: self-adhesive film. This adheres to almost any surface and has the additional advantage of being easy to move. As I said before, though, you have to make sure to get the right markers.

> **Practical Tip**
>
> If you use Super Stickies on whiteboards, you might find they leave a light trace of adhesive, which can make the board difficult to clean later. So here you are better off using normal sticky notes (thanks to Christoph Pater for this tip).

To make a long story short: either use Super Stickies or self-adhesive film. There's little point in using anything else. These are the only materials that will leave you well equipped for the retrospective.

2.3.3 The Right Flipchart Paper

You have a few things to consider when choosing flipchart paper. You often find a flipchart easel available but no paper, or flipchart paper is available, but it's all been written on, so you have to write on the back. I have nothing against saving money or being environmentally friendly, but you can't beat clean, blank flipchart paper.

Good flipchart paper meets three criteria. It is:

- Squared
- Perforated
- Blank

Unlined and non-squared flipchart paper options aren't ideal, particularly if you don't have a lot of experience making good use of flipchart paper to display ideas. Blank paper might be great if you're looking to draw something and the lines would only get in the way. In a retrospective, though, you want to record ideas, and a few guiding lines can be quite helpful. For example, if you don't want your lines of text sagging down the right side, guiding lines will help you keep your text horizontal. Even if you want to sketch something, the lines are the basis. Whenever possible, insist on squared flipchart paper.

> **Practical Tip**
> Before the retrospective, make sure you have enough flipchart paper.

Non-perforated flipchart paper is completely impractical. It works well if all you want to do is keep turning over the page, but in a good retrospective, you want to tear each page off the pad. Take the agenda, for example. Keeping the agenda on permanent display is important. To do this, you have to be able to tear the page off the pad and stick it to the wall. You can easily tear non-perforated paper down the middle rather than along the top, thus destroying your work. This is so avoidable. If you want to use a flipchart in your retrospective, insist on the right paper.

> **Practical Tip**
> Always have a roll of painter's tape or masking tape for hanging flipchart paper up around the room. Painter's tape is good because it's the easiest way to get things up on the wall and it can also be removed without damaging the paintwork.

2.4 Food

A good retrospective needs to include something to eat. Have you ever been to a wedding without food? Have you ever been to a birthday party without a cake? What's watching football on TV without chips and beer? Wherever people get together, there is usually something to eat. People love to talk and get to know each other over good food. So why not provide something to eat at your retrospectives? I'm not talking about three-course meals, just little things like some fruit, nuts, gummy bears. or pretzels. The benefits are huge—they include:

- A relaxed atmosphere
- Better results
- Increased popularity of your retrospectives

- Fewer late participants
- Less stomach rumbling

If you don't believe me, try it out. By the way, this isn't just a good idea for retrospectives; it works well in all kinds of meeting.

2.5 The Agenda

Meetings with no agenda are largely ineffective. Most often, they turn into mere discussions that produce no implementable results and are simply a waste of everyone's time. The beauty of retrospectives is that they come with their own framework for the agenda— the six phases outlined in section 1.3. All you have to do is breathe life into that framework with activities from the sources listed in section 1.4. In choosing, make sure that the activities can be carried out effectively with the number of participants attending and that you have all the necessary materials. You also have to familiarize yourself with the details of the activities you choose. Knowing the goal of each activity, how long they should last, and how best to carry them out is important.

Years ago, I wanted to use the fishbone activity in one of my retrospectives. This is a useful activity for the Generate Insights phase. I hadn't worked with the technique before and assumed it worked like a mind map. However, when I tried to explain the activity during the retrospective I realized that something wasn't quite right. In the end, I had to look it up in Derby and Larsen's book [1] while the whole team sat waiting. It wasn't exactly terrible but wasn't particularly professional either. If you were to do this for each activity, your retrospectives would take twice as long.

To carry out a retrospective well, you must be prepared. You must know the activities inside out so that you can answer any questions the team might have. Knowing the activities well is also vital if you are going to do the most important part of your job as facilitator: help the team to use the activity effectively to get results. When you understand an activity fully, you can ask the right questions and guide the participants through the retrospective. Sometimes, though, you must be willing to scratch an activity completely and try something you feel would better fit the current situation.

After you've chosen the activities, you can put the agenda together. That includes the name and amount of time planned for each step. Send the agenda out to the participants at the same time as the invitation to the retrospective. That lets people know what's coming and allows them to prepare properly for the retrospective. During the retrospective, make sure the agenda is clearly visible throughout the room. Best practice is to tick off each of the points on the agenda as you deal with them. You can see an example of an agenda in Figure 2-1.

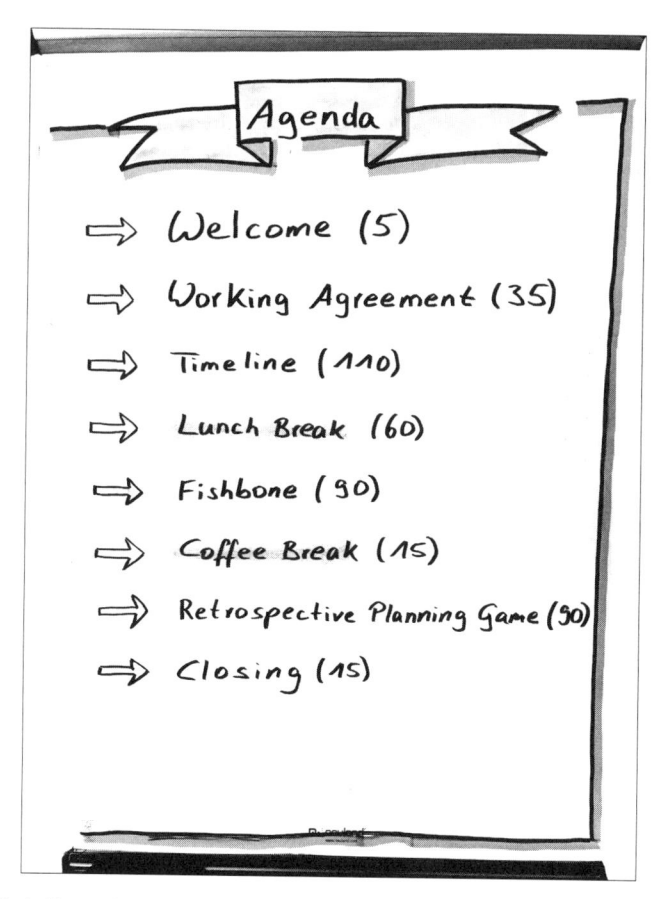

```
Agenda
⇨ Welcome (5)
⇨ Working Agreement (35)
⇨ Timeline (110)
⇨ Lunch Break (60)
⇨ Fishbone (90)
⇨ Coffee Break (15)
⇨ Retrospective Planning Game (90)
⇨ Closing (15)
```

Figure 2-1 Example of a retrospective's agenda

Summary

Louis Pasteur said that "fortune favors only the prepared mind." Good preparation is the foundation of good retrospectives. Like a good jazz musician, only when you are well prepared you are able to improvise. A musician knows the music inside out and has practiced his scales for the various chords thousands of times. Only then can he play a good, coherent solo without having to think about every single note.

Good preparation means you can tackle your retrospectives with the same confidence as the master musician, thus making the atmosphere more relaxed and more creative. Time invested in preparation always pays off. Here is a summary of the important points:

- Make sure that you've clarified all the important questions in advance.
- Make sure that the room is as well fitted out as possible.
- Make sure you have the right quality materials in the right quantity.
- Ensure that there is something for the participants to snack on.
- Last, but not least: Make sure you have prepared a meaningful agenda with clear timeframes and activities that are appropriate to the participants and the retrospective.

Reference

[1] Esther Derby and Diana Larsen. 2006. *Agile Retrospectives: Making Good Teams Great*. O'Reilly UK Ltd.

3

The First Retrospective

As the saying goes: There's a first time for everything. I imagine that you are reading this book because you are looking to lead at least one retrospective. If you already have some experience in leading retrospectives and you know the retrospective's phase model, you can skip this chapter. If you don't have experience, in this chapter I take you step by step through your first retrospective so that you find your first retrospective easier than I did mine. To do this, I've made a few assumptions:

- Your retrospective will last an hour.
- You will have three to eight participants.
- Your retrospective will consider a relatively short period of time (one to four weeks maximum).
- Your room for the retrospective has a flipchart and/or a whiteboard.

3.1 Preparation

The following list contains all the materials you'll need for your first retrospective:

- A flipchart or whiteboard and the appropriate markers
- Enough pens for the participants (ballpoint pens will do)
- Two pads of sticky notes
- Circular stickers
- Gummy bears

You must set the agenda for your retrospective before sending out the invitation. Here is a sample agenda you can use to make your life easier:

- Set the stage: Car Comparison **(5 min.)**
- Gather data: Mad, Sad, Glad **(15 min.)**
- Generate Insights: The 5 Whys **(20 min.)**
- Define next experiments and hypotheses: Brainstorming **(15 min.)**
- Closing: ROTI **(5 min.)**

It goes without saying that the times given are only an example and should be adapted according to your needs. You will also notice that this agenda is missing the Check Hypothesis phase. This is because I'm assuming that either this is your very first retrospective or that you didn't define hypotheses in your previous retrospective.

After your agenda is ready, you can send the invitation out to your participants. Don't forget to book the room, preferably including fifteen to thirty minutes before the start time, so you have a chance to prepare the space.

> **Practical Tip**
> The longer you have access to the room before the retrospective, the better. This gives you enough time to fix any problems. It is possible you'll find the room in a completely desolate state.

Make sure that you've organized something to eat for the day of the retrospective. Given that this retrospective only lasts an hour, a bag of gummy bears should do it (see the earlier materials list). Get the room prepared before the actual retrospective starts. Set up the furniture to make cooperative work as easy as possible. My favorite setups are "table islands" (two tables pushed together) and the classic circle of chairs.

Every participant gets a pen and a few sticky notes. You should always have one pad of sticky notes in reserve. The bag of gummy bears goes in the middle of the workspace. Then write your agenda on a piece of flipchart paper and post it, so it's clearly visible throughout the room. This ensures that everyone will be able to see the agenda and that you can still use the flipchart during the retrospective (if you don't have a whiteboard available).

If you're still not very familiar with the activities you've chosen for each phase, use any remaining time to read through them again. Then you're ready to go.

3.2 Set the Stage: Car Comparison

After all participants are present, you can start the retrospective. Begin by greeting everyone and briefly explaining the agenda. If the team has a charter, remind them of the rules for cooperative work that they've developed. If the team has no charter, skip this step; you don't have enough time to deal with this in a single hour retrospective. In such a case, however, set up a workshop in the near future that will be dedicated to creating a team charter. Alternatively, plan more time into your next retrospective and take care of it then.

> **Practical Tip**
> If you find that not all participants are punctual, make use of the n–1 rule: you start the retrospective if all participants (n) except one (–1) are present. This way you can usually start on time without having to wait for notorious latecomers.

Now ask the participants to compare the period you're considering to a car. Everyone should use just a few words to describe what kind of car this period makes him think of. Giving one or two examples of how this might sound is best—for example, "a rusty old VW Passat" or "a top-class Lamborghini Murciélago." The participants needn't follow a fixed order, but make sure that everybody says something. Let the group members decide for themselves in which order to respond. Don't judge or comment on the answers. Every contribution should simply be warmly welcomed.

> **Practical Tip**
>
> When some people use these more playful approaches in their workshops for the first time, they worry that the group will find the activities ridiculous and refuse to join in. In my experience, this is extremely rare. Remember that as the facilitator, you set the tone. Introduce these activities in a professional and sincere way and, in most cases, everyone will take part. If somebody questions the activity, simply ask him to join in. You can also offer to explain the purpose of the activity in more detail after the retrospective. If the person still refuses to take part, let him know he is free to leave the room at any time.

3.3 Gather Data

After the car comparison, jump straight into the next phase: Gather Data. Your activity, "Mad, Sad, Glad," is easy to explain. Each participant uses his sticky notes to record all the things that made him mad, sad, or glad during the time being considered. Additionally, members can use the field with the flower in the lower-right area, to say "Thank you" to one or more team members. As you briefly explain the activity, draw a large cross on the whiteboard or flipchart and label the resulting four areas as in Figure 3-1.

Before you begin the activity, check that the participants understand and answer any questions. Remind them to write as legibly as possible and include only one idea per sticky note. Now you can get started.

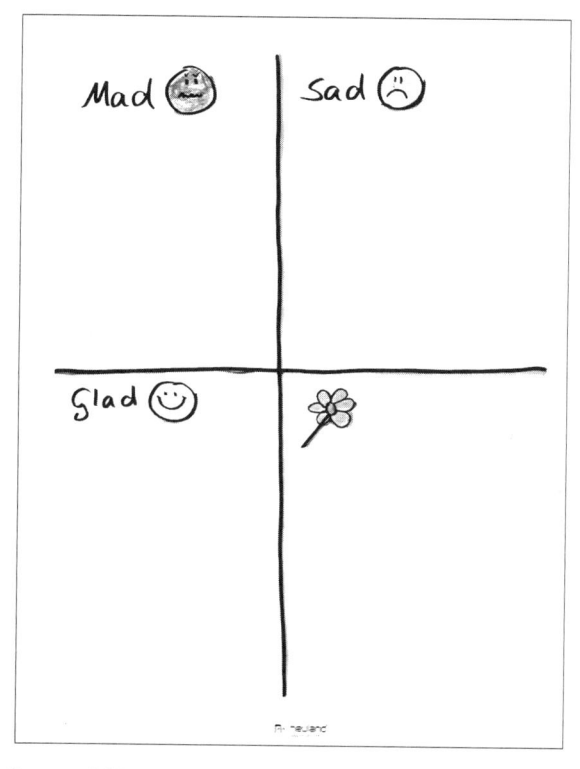

Figure 3-1 Prepared flipchart for the Mad, Sad, and Glad activity

> **Practical Tip**
>
> While the participants write diligently on their sticky notes, your job as facilitator is to ask questions about the four categories to give the participants a few ideas. Here are some examples:
>
> - What did you enjoy in recent weeks?
> - What kept happening that drove you mad?
> - What happened that you are glad about?
> - What frustrated you?
> - What delightful thing did a colleague do for you?
>
> These questions are a helpful way to keep the writing going if you feel that the team has stalled.

Use the last 5 minutes to briefly read out all the sticky notes and get any clarification you need from the authors. Call a halt to the writing in plenty of time for this review. As you go through the sticky notes, group them by theme. In most cases, this grouping will begin to give you an idea of the most pressing problems.

You now have two options for helping the participants to choose the topics that will be their focus for the rest of the retrospective:

- Distribute the circular stickers and have the participants use them to vote for two topics (dot voting).
- Simply choose the two topics that are represented by the two largest groups of sticky notes.

Practical Tip

It is important, especially in the case of short retrospectives, that you do not exceed the time planned for each phase. Of course, this means you won't be able to discuss everything that comes up, and that's fine. You can be sure that the participants will come up with the most important issues first. You can only hope to produce usable results if you keep to the timebox. Doing this will also show your participants that you keep to the agenda and that even in short retrospectives, achieving good results is possible. As a facilitator, keeping an eye on the time and regularly letting the groups know how much time they have left for an activity is important. If you have the capability, project a timer on the wall for each phase. You can find software for this for all common operating systems (such as XNote Stopwatch for Windows). You can also use a big clock that is visible to everyone (such as a Time Timer clock).

If you go for the circular stickers variant, give each participant three stickers that he can place next to the three topics that seem most valuable to investigate. Then count the number of stickers per group of sticky notes and write this figure next to the group. The two groups with the most stickers are the winners and are the topics to be discussed in the following phases of the retrospective.

3.4 Generate Insights: 5 Whys

As I wrote in the first chapter, the 5-Why method is a technique that is already more than 100 years old. The idea behind this technique is that most things that seem to be obvious causes of problems are only symptoms and that the root of the problem is much deeper. The 5 Whys helps you find the root cause of problems by repeating the question "Why?" at least five times.

Here is a simple example: Suppose you develop cars and your problem is that nobody buys them. The following is a series of questions you might ask:

- Why does nobody buy our cars? Because dealers won't stock them.
- Why won't dealers stock the cars? Because no dealers want to sell them.
- Why don't dealers want to sell the cars? Because the cars have a bad reputation with potential buyers.
- Why do the cars have a bad reputation with buyers? Because they performed very poorly in the latest round of crash testing.
- Why did the cars do so badly? Because thus far we have failed to consider the issue of safety.

Of course, this is a highly simplified example, but it gives you a feel for how the technique works. Finding a single answer to a why question is not always possible; sometimes there are several causes which, in turn, can have several further causes. This is completely normal.

Here is an additional example from the area of software development:

- Why did we start the ... meeting too late? The room was not available.
- Why wasn't the room available? Forgot to put room in the schedule.
- Why did we forget it? Peter always does it, and he was ill.
- Why does Peter always schedule the room? Because it is easy to have Peter doing it.
- Why do we think it is easy to have only one person doing a task...

Divide the participants into two groups, if appropriate. Each of the groups will work on one of the topics chosen in the previous phase. Give each group a piece of flipchart paper, which they will use to document their results.

> **Practical Tip**
> If you feel that the activity is unclear or the group is stalled, sit down and join the groups alternately. In my experience, people are far more willing to ask questions when you are sitting with the group.

Plan for a few minutes at the end of this phase for the two groups to present their results. To do this, one member of each group goes to the front of the room, displays the piece of flipchart paper, and briefly explains the results. As in the other phases, make sure that you keep to the times stated on the agenda.

3.5 Define Next Experiments: Brainstorming

Most participants already have some ideas on how work can be improved when they come to a retrospective. The preceding phases of the retrospective have also built a foundation for more ideas. At this point, participants are either even more convinced that their original idea would work or they have come to realize that perhaps it isn't such a good idea after all. It might also be the case that participants feel their ideas are still good but don't help to solve the current most pressing problem. Ideas in this category can be saved for the next retrospective.

The Brainstorming activity makes use of the participant's wealth of ideas. Each participant now has five minutes to come up with a maximum of three ideas for possible experiments that he feels have the highest potential for positive change. We limit the number to three because otherwise, you might not have enough time to go through all of them. The participants write their ideas on sticky notes, keeping to the one experiment per note rule. The sticky notes are then stuck up on an open bit of wall. When the five minutes are up, each person explains his idea(s) in a few words. This explanation should include what he believes the effect of his experiment will be; that is, his hypothesis. Participants should try to group the ideas as they post them. You are still in brainstorming mode so avoid discussing or judging the ideas presented. Again, employ the circular stickers, this time to choose the idea that has the greatest potential for success.

Agree on only one idea. This might seem odd given that you have the whole team now highly motivated to try out a bunch of ideas. But if you want to make sure that work is actually done, agreeing on only one idea is essential. After all, you want your first retrospective to be a success. Make it clear to the participants that the idea they've chosen is essentially an experiment. You can have an idea of what the effect may be, but nobody can be sure. So, it is important now to add a hypothesis to the experiment you've chosen. Make sure that this hypothesis is verifiable. Otherwise, you're wasting your time. You are now laying the foundation for the next retrospective, at which you will compare the original hypothesis with what actually happened in the experiment.

> **Practical Tip**
>
> Many teams make their experiments too imprecise or too big to define. Thus, their experiments haven't been carried out by the time of the next retrospective. To avoid this frustration, familiarize the participants with the concept of SMART goals. SMART stands for:
>
> - **S**pecific (simple, sensible, significant)
> - **M**easurable (meaningful, motivating)
> - **A**chievable (agreed, attainable)
> - **R**elevant (reasonable, realistic, and resourced)
> - **T**ime-bound (time-based, time limited)
>
> All the experiments chosen should meet these criteria. They should be specific. So, no nebulous, incomprehensible experiments, but concrete, specific, and directly executable. They should be measurable. You can only be sure that experiment has been carried out if you can measure it. They should be achievable. That is, they should be small enough to be carried out within a few days' or weeks' time. Ensure, too, that the group has the power to carry out the experiments. That the experiments should be relevant to the current issues goes without saying. Say it anyway. Finally, experiments should be time-bound. Define a clear timeframe in which the experiment is to be carried out. Experiments that meet these criteria are much more likely to be successful.

Now all that is left to do is determine who will be responsible for carrying out the experiment and when this will happen. The person made responsible doesn't necessarily have to carry out the experiment by himself. In this case, responsibility simply refers to making sure that the experiment is actually carried out.

3.6 Closing: ROTI

You've come to the end of your first retrospective. This is a good time to thank all the participants for their work and explain what is going to happen to the results:

- You'll take photos of all the work produced and distribute them to the participants. How you do that is up to you. One possible way is to put them on a flipchart and put it on the wall of your team's room.
- The ideas that were not chosen form part of what's called an "improvement backlog." All the ideas produced have value and shouldn't simply be thrown away. The best place for them is on the wall in the team room.

Now let the participants know that at the next retrospective you will all be reviewing the hypotheses you've created today. Also, let them know when that next retrospective will be held. The only thing left for you to do now is to hold a retrospective on the retrospective. A short ROTI analysis (see Section 1.3.6 "Return on Time Invested") will get this job done.

Summary

Congratulations—you've made it to the end of your first retrospective. Now you've laid the foundation for many more successful retrospectives. This chapter gave you all the info and tools to start right away. Now it is up to you. Invite your team, reserve a room, get some food, prepare the agenda, and you are ready to go. The more you practice, the better you'll get, as always. Enjoy the ride.

In the following chapters, we will further deepen your knowledge.

4

The Retrospective Facilitator

The role of the retrospective facilitator is very important. The facilitator can tip the balance when it comes to the success of a retrospective. However, if you're attentive to a few things and work at it, facilitation can be a lot of fun. The goal of this chapter is to explain what you need to become a good facilitator and give you the basics. In this book, I can only touch upon many of the topics, but after this chapter, you'll have a good foundation on which to build.

4.1 How Do I Become a Good Facilitator?

The answer to how to become a good facilitator is quite simple: practice, practice, practice. No one is born a master. Some facilitators do make it look like the easiest thing in the world, but in reality, it requires a great deal of background knowledge and heaps of experience. From my point of view, a very good facilitator has the following skills:

- Is a good listener
- Has a feel for when a discussion is still goal-oriented or when it should be interrupted
- Makes sure that everyone has an opportunity to speak
- Makes sure that all opinions on a topic are heard
- Helps to make decisions
- Is well prepared
- Is confident, flexible, respectful, and authentic

- Creates an atmosphere in which everyone feels safe
- Tackles conflict constructively
- Has a sense of humor
- Keeps the energy level up during a workshop
- Asks the right questions
- Visualizes the input of the workshop's participants
- Stays neutral, but can also question the team's assumptions

As you can see, it's a long list, and I know very few facilitators who meet all the criteria. Some of the criteria, like a sense of humor, are hard to learn. Some people simply have a natural talent for these things. But even talented facilitators must practice. Like most things in life, most of the skills on the preceding list can be learned over time.

If you want to become a good facilitator, you must know where your strengths and weaknesses lie and continually work to improve. Of course, the best way to improve is by leading as many workshops as possible. Alongside this experience, you can further your development by taking courses and reading books on facilitation. Everything you learn can be deployed in the next workshop and refined. Thus, little by little, you can improve your skills in this very enjoyable area.

A full introduction to the topic of facilitation would exceed the scope of this book. However, in this chapter, I'll give you a brief introduction to the topic, as well as a few tips on some problems that typically occur in retrospectives.

When you look at the fourteen skills on the list, you'll realize that most of them can only be practiced if you're a good listener. That is why good listening is a facilitator's most important skill. Unfortunately, listening is a skill that is losing more and more value in our society. One of the main reasons for this is the increased number of forms of documentation that exist today: written documentation (e-books), for example, or audio recordings (MP3 or other digital formats). In the past, if you wanted to re-tell a story that was told to you, you had to listen carefully when you heard it. Stories were passed on from generation to generation over centuries in just that way. Today, most of these stories are found in books, and you can simply read them. In the past, when musicians came into a town or village it was a big event because people only seldom had the chance to hear a good singer or instrumentalist. Today, there are recordings of these singers that you can listen to again and again. Because we no longer need to listen the first time, our society values good listening less than in the past.

Julian Treasure gave an interesting TED Talk [1] at the end of which he gave five tips on how to improve your listening skills:

- To regularly calibrate your hearing, you should spend three minutes a day in as quiet a place as possible.
- If you're in a very loud place, you should try to identify the individual noises. Where are the sounds coming from? Who is making the sounds?
- You should concentrate on everyday noises and try to enjoy them—the sound of your coffee machine or tumble dryer, for example. You should try to recognize patterns in these sounds.
- You should listen in different ways: actively, passively, critically, empathically, and so on. Also, become conscious of the differences.
- Finally, he introduced an acronym: RASA (Receive, Appreciate, Summarize, Ask). Always go through these four steps when listening to someone.

These five tips are a good starting point for consciously retraining your hearing. This is enormously important, as many of the techniques of a good facilitator are based exactly on the skill of listening.

In his book, *Facilitator's Guide to Participatory Decision Making* [2], Sam Kaner introduces 18 techniques for facilitators that are connected to listening. In the next sections, I would like to go somewhat deeper into some of them.

> **Practical Tip**
> To start with, pick just one or two of the techniques described next and practice them in your next retrospective and, potentially, also in other meetings. Only when you feel that you've mastered these should you take up the next technique.

4.1.1 Respect Different Communication Styles

People communicate in the most different ways, above all when laying out their ideas. Sadly, there are some communication styles that go down less well and that can deter people from listening. Because of this, sometimes even what might be the best of ideas remain unheard. Fewer good ideas are preferred because a participant cannot express himself particularly well. Unfortunately, many communications styles put most people off. Here are some examples of how discussion participants might use these off-putting communication styles:

- Continually repeating themselves
- Continually grinding to a halt through shyness or nerves
- Going overboard when presenting their viewpoint or adding irrelevant comments
- Suddenly wanting to take the discussion in a completely different direction
- Showing very strong emotions openly

Groups that are better able to accommodate these communication styles get a wider bandwidth of ideas and suggestions and thus, in the end, a better result. The key to this improved ability is, as always, the facilitator. Here are some examples of how a facilitator can improve communication in a group:

- If someone constantly repeats himself, the facilitator paraphrases to help the person summarize his point of view.

- With nervous participants, the facilitator can help by asking open questions (without steering in a particular direction).
- The facilitator can help participants who seem to want to start a whole new discussion by asking them to clarify how this new point fits into the present discussion [2, p. 43].

In any event, treating every participant with respect by listening carefully and, if necessary, by helping them to express themselves is always important. Of course, listening to each other is important, too.

4.1.2 Paraphrasing

The word *paraphrasing* comes from Greek and means "to outline" or "to give again in your words." Paraphrasing is one of the facilitator's most powerful and direct techniques because it shows the speaker very clearly that you have been actively listening. You can also use this technique to make sure that you have fully understood everything that was said. This is especially important when a speaker is expressing himself in a tangled and confusing way, and what he's trying to say is not clear.

Paraphrasing is quite simple. Repeat what you have understood in your words. Afterward, always check that what you heard was what the speaker meant. Do this by asking, for example, "Have I understood that right?" or "Was it that what you wanted to say?" If you have misunderstood, ask the speaker to say it again more clearly. Keep doing this until you have correctly repeated his point of view or idea.

4.1.3 Support Participants

Sometimes, a person has problems clearly expressing his idea, or a statement is so confusing as to be incomprehensible. In such cases, the facilitator's job is to ask the speaker targeted questions to help him make his ideas comprehensible. Here are some possible questions:

- Could you give us an example?
- How come?
- What do you mean by...?
- Could you draw that for me?

With these and similar questions, you, as the facilitator, can help to get a clear picture of the idea.

4.1.4 Stacking

Always use the stacking technique when more than one participant wants to speak at the same time. This technique prevents people from trying to talk over one another and is also useful when you have an especially dominant team member who would prefer to talk the whole time and prevent others from getting a word in. The way it works is quite simple:

- You say: "Everyone who has something to say about that, please raise your hands."
- Then you decide the running order; that is, "Paul, you first, then Sonja, and third Sven."
- After Paul is finished, you give the floor to Sonja and then Sven, and so on.
- When everyone has spoken, you again ask whether anyone has something to say about the topic. If there are more, start again from step 2.

Whoever has the floor has the exclusive right to speak. You make sure that he is not interrupted. Use this technique to make sure that everyone who has something to say gets the opportunity. An added benefit is that the whole discussion is calmer, and the participants are in a better position to actually listen, instead of just waiting for a break in the flow of the talk to jam in their opinion.

4.1.5 Encourage

The encourage technique is used primarily when the facilitator has the feeling that a few participants are holding back and leaving the work to the others, or are naturally more introverted. When you encourage, you deliberately ask for other points of view, ideas, or comments, so that the quieter participants are also invited to the discussion. Here are some examples:

- Who else has an idea?
- Can someone give me an example of this point of view?
- Would someone who hasn't spoken yet like to comment on this?
- Are there any questions about this topic?
- How could we get to the heart of this?
- Who wants to play devil's advocate for this idea?

The goal of each of these questions is to give someone the opportunity to make his opinion heard. They are like a cross in soccer when the ball is passed across the goal mouth so that the ball need only be tapped in to score. I have often seen how questions like these can inspire someone to speak when until that point he had only been silent.

4.1.6 Feedback Emotion

Lots of people have a problem showing their emotions. Emotions, though, are an important part of human communication and therefore must also be considered. Above all, our emotions have a direct effect on the other participants of a workshop or retrospective. Address emotions head on, or you might unwittingly ignore them. As a facilitator, constantly be aware of the emotional mood, especially in conversations and discussions that deal with difficult topics. If you notice a strong emotion, the first step is to feed it back in the form of a question. Then, go back to listening carefully and supporting the participants as they answer the question. Here are a few examples of emotional feedback questions:

- It sounds to me as if you're worried/concerned. Am I right?
- I can hear in your voice that you are [angry, frustrated, sad, happy, content, and so on].
- I get the feeling that this situation is overwhelming for you. Is that true?

In the beginning, talking about feelings will feel odd, especially in those teams that are uncomfortable with emotions. The more often you do it, though, the more it will become a normal part of future discussions. Teams that can work with their emotions are, as a rule, more successful than teams that cannot.

4.1.7 Intended Silence

I am a person who had extreme difficulty staying silent. This is especially the case when I'm alone with someone whom I don't yet know very well. I've been getting better at it over the last few years, though. In the meantime, I've come so far that I have learned to treasure intended silence.

Most people feel uncomfortable when silence suddenly descends in the middle of the discussion. It feels odd at the beginning when no one speaks, and everyone is waiting for something to happen. Experience has shown, though, that when the facilitator can manage to endure the silence, most of the other participants can, too. Silence during a discussion can be very valuable. Perhaps someone is about to speak and just needs a few seconds to get his thoughts in order. Or someone has said something unusual, and you all need a few seconds to take it in.

In a situation like that, concentrate on the speakers. Don't say anything, not even "hm" or "aha," and don't nod your head. If necessary, raise your hand, just in case anyone wants to break the silence.

You'll be amazed at what can come of welcoming these moments of silence and letting them sink in.

4.1.8 Listen for Common Ground

Use Common Ground technique whenever different parties in a discussion take completely different points of view. When this happens, there is often an overarching commonality that unites the parties. The facilitator's task is to look for this common ground and report it back to the participants. This happens in four steps:

- Summarize the discussion. For example, "Let me summarize what I've heard from both parties. I've heard a lot of differences, but also one or two similarities."
- Continue by articulating the difference: "It sounds as though, at Christmas time, one group wants to go home earlier, whereas the other group would prefer to take a few days holiday."
- Then come to the common ground: "So it looks as though both groups want to work a little less during that period."
- Check-in: "Am I seeing that correctly?"

Finding this common ground is not always easy. When you can manage it, though, it is a very good foundation for further discussion and a possible compromise. Mastering this technique improves your chances of finding solutions in muddled situations.

4.2 Visual Facilitation

Visual facilitation is a technique for leading successful workshops as well as retrospectives. Simply put, it's about accompanying the workshop visually. This starts with your preparation when you use the flipchart to visualize the agenda. Much more important, however, is to visually support the group in their work: by making the stated visible, for example, or giving the team opportunities to work visually.

Many people believe that visual facilitation must involve very artistic drawings and that to use the technique you have to be good at drawing. Quite apart from the fact everyone can draw something and that it is a skill that can be learned, what is most important is not the quality of the drawing, but making the information that is discussed in a workshop visible. It can just be a comment made by a participant written on a sticky note and stuck on the wall, or a simple drawing that depicts a current process. Simple things like these help to forge a common understanding of the topic being discussed. I have often witnessed groups discuss an issue at length until they were all able to visualize it and then settle on a common language to describe it. Working with pictures and visual metaphors allows you to explain a lot of things more easily.

Flipcharts or whiteboards are in ever more conference rooms. This makes it all the more amazing that these tools continue to be left on the sidelines. Even when they are used, the results often lack structure and are illegible. I still find it remarkable just what affects you can achieve with the simplest methods and structures, such as flipcharts. You can learn the basic skills in about hour and then it's just a question of practice. When you've practiced for a bit, it gets ever easier, and in the end, you'll feel the benefit in every one of your meetings.

4.2.1 The 1×1 of Visual Structure

If you keep to a few simple rules, structuring a flipchart so that it's easy to read and also looks good is not rocket science. You can learn the fundamentals of visual structure, for use principally with flipcharts, by sticking to the following ground rules:

- Draw and write in black. Other colors come later.
- Draw a frame to contain everything.
- Write text in text boxes.
- First, write the text, then draw the box afterward.
- For rectangular text boxes, draw all the sides individually.

- Don't ever draw through letters. Instead, break the line.
- Avoid BLOCK CAPITALS.
- Improve your handwriting.
- Use visualizations that are easy to draw.
- Use crayons to fill the boxes.

4.2.1.1 Draw and Write in Black

When you begin, write and draw everything in black. You could equate it with the templates in a coloring book. The black lines give you the structure, and the colors come later and bring life to your drawing. A general rule for the number of colors to use is black and two additional colors. The only exception is gray. You can always use gray to bring shading into the visualization. Some facilitators prefer to write everything in blue, and there's nothing wrong with that. A further advantage of drawing everything in black is that you don't have to think about which color would work best. You can then finish the drawing when you have time—when the participants are busy with something else, for example, or after the retrospective has finished.

> **Practical Tip**
>
> Don't use any water-based markers for this step. Their ink can smudge later when you want to add shading or colors. Instead, use outliners.

> **Practical Tip**
>
> If you're leading a longer workshop and you know that you'll be using the flipchart preparing a few sheets of flipchart paper in advance is a good idea. You can do this even if you don't yet know the headings you'll put at the top of each sheet. Doing this in advance means that you avoid having the participants sit and look on as you draw a frame on a flipchart during the retrospective.

4.2.1.2 Draw a Frame

You wouldn't believe the difference that drawing a frame on a flipchart makes. Just the addition of the frame makes the content of the flipchart look more structured. It sets out clear boundaries as to where the contents begin and where they end and thus sets the focus on what is most important.

In Figure 4-1 you see a template of a flipchart. It already has a frame, and there is enough space for the title. Prepare 5–10 flipcharts like this, and you'll have automatically less to stress about during the retrospective itself.

Figure 4-1 Flipchart template

4.2.1.3 Write Text in Text Boxes

You don't need to pack all text into text boxes, but important elements like headings should always be in text boxes. They help to emphasize and structure important contents. Text in a text box simply always looks better. A text box can be any shape you like, from simple rectangles, circles, or ovals to special shapes like banners, arrows, or speech bubbles. In Figure 4-2 you can see an example of the use of text boxes. As well as the text boxes, I have included little symbols in this drawing to give the drawing more context and to make the whole thing a bit more relaxed. The more flipcharts like this that you make, the more fun it becomes.

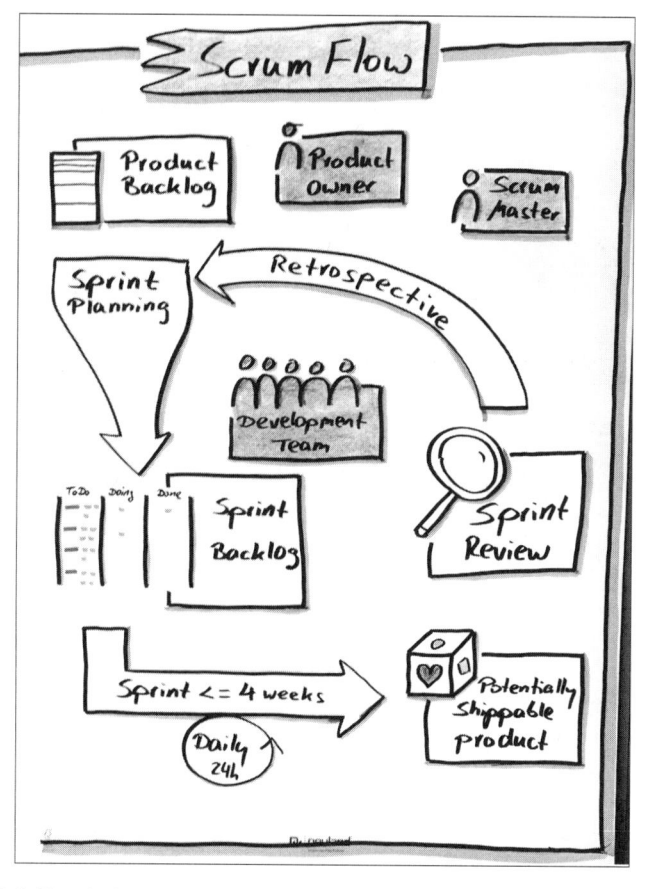

Figure 4-2 Text in boxes

4.2.1.4 Text First

When you want to put text in a text box, always write the text itself first. This is the only way you can be sure that the text will fit inside the box. Squeezing text into a small box looks just ugly (see Figure 4-3) as small text lost in a big box. So always think to yourself: first the text, then the box.

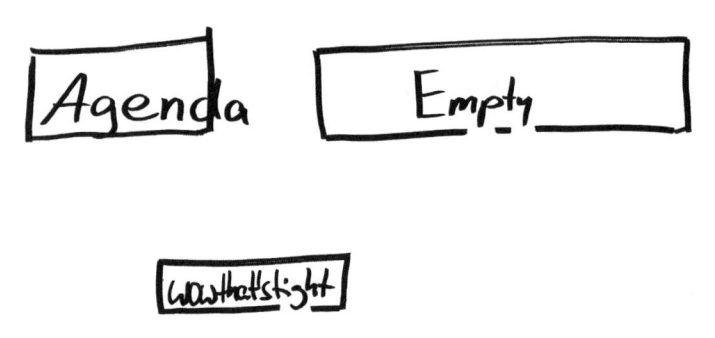

Figure 4-3 Ugly text boxes

> **Practical Tip**
> Draw the box for the text immediately after you have written the text. If you fill the rest of the chart with text first, finding room for the text boxes as well will be difficult. This is especially true if you want to use a more unusual text box, like a banner.

4.2.1.5 Draw Sides Individually

When drawing a rectangle, it is always best to deliberately draw each side individually, thus making sure that the finished shape looks like a rectangle. Otherwise, you run the risk of it looking more like a circle (see Figure 4-4). This is a simple tip that has a big effect.

It's always when you're in a hurry when you want to get your ideas on the flipchart or whiteboard quickly that you fall into the trap of drawing all the sides with a single stroke. Take the appropriate time, and your drawings will be both legible and easier to understand. Also, you'll have more time in which to formulate your ideas better.

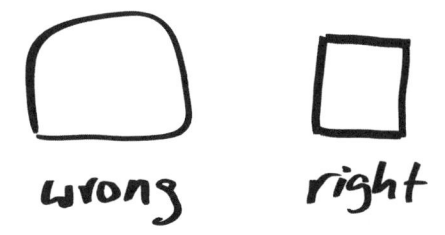

Figure 4-4 Always draw the sides individually

4.2.1.6 Never Draw Through Letters

The reason for not drawing through letters is very simple: It looks better, and the letters are easier to read. Have a look at the difference (see Figure 4-5).

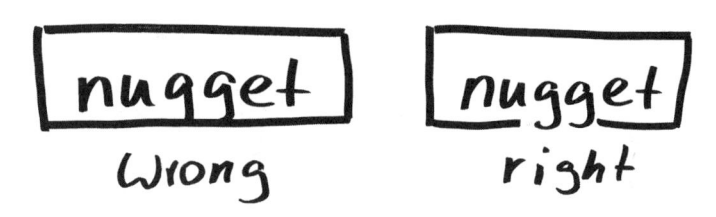

Figure 4-5 Never draw through letters

The upper nugget looks quite jammed in whereas the other has plenty of room to dangle its "legs."

4.2.1.7 Avoid BLOCK CAPITALS

Like the previous tip, this one is primarily aesthetic: avoiding block capitals looks better. Also, capital letters are often used to indicate a loud voice. If you use block capitals everywhere, it looks as though the whole flipchart is shouting. Of course, you can use capitals when you want to emphasize a particular text. You can also use them in headings, though a text box works better in my opinion.

4.2.1.8 Use Crayons to Fill the Text Boxes

This tip is again primarily aesthetic: Use crayons to fill your text boxes. As you can see in Figure 4-6, crayons give your drawings a final touch. Additionally, you can add some context by using different colors to indicate elements that belong together.

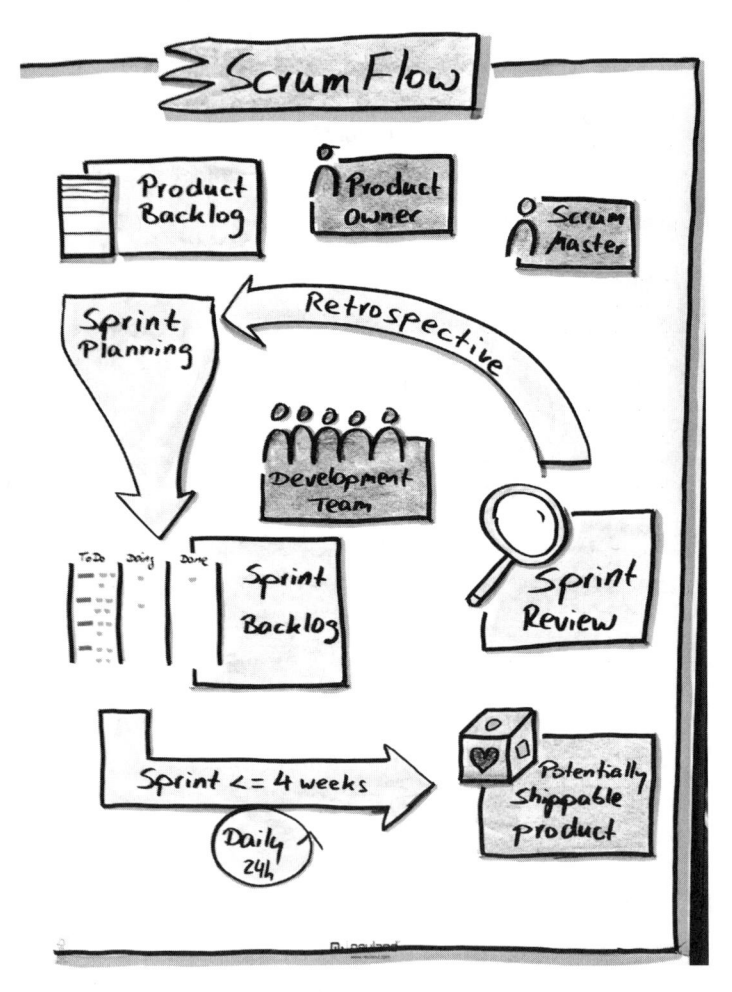

Figure 4-6 Use crayons to fill text boxes

> **Practical Tip**
>
> Work on your handwriting, because illegible visualizations are more than annoying. What's the point of visualizations if you have to make an effort to decode them? You can destroy your work with sloppy handwriting. Learn moderator's handwriting: The hand rests on the paper, letters are proportional and close together, but not overlapping. Don't let the group behind you drive you crazy; take the time to write cleanly. The more often you practice this, the faster you will get at writing with moderator's handwriting.

> **Practical Tip**
>
> All the symbols, text boxes, and other elements that you want to use in the visualization should be easy for you to draw. Start with a small set of elements and slowly add new ones. Practice new elements often enough that you know exactly how best to draw them. That way, you can be sure that you're able to draw your elements quickly and that meetings won't grind to a halt because of your visual facilitation.

4.3 Visual Retrospectives

Many retrospective facilitators have already considered how to use visual aids in retrospectives. In the following sections, I present a few of these special visualizations for retrospectives.

4.3.1 The Speedboat Retrospective

The speedboat retrospective is among my favorite visualizations. It was one of the first variations I used myself. The idea of the speedboat comes from Luke Hohmann's book, *Innovation Games: Creating Breakthrough Products Through Collaborative Play* [3], that introduces the speedboat as one of his innovation games.

> **Practical Tip**
> Draw the speedboat before the retrospective. That way, you have enough time to draw a nice boat and can use your time more effectively during the retrospective itself.

Hohmann's idea is to use this visualization to depict all the things that a client doesn't like about their product or service. To start, he draws a speedboat floating on the surface of the sea. The speedboat is a metaphor that represents the product or service. It wants to go forward as quickly as possible but is held back or delayed by different anchors in the water under the boat. The object of the speedboat simulation is to attach these anchors onto the boat. This is most often done with sticky notes to represent the anchors (see Figure 4-7). An anchor chain is then drawn from each anchor (sticky note) to the boat. All the things that prevent the speedboat from moving forward can thus be represented.

After collecting all the anchors, discuss each anchor with the client to get a feel for which of the anchors represent the biggest drags or delays. The product team can then use this information to improve their products and services.

You follow a similar approach when using the speedboat in a retrospective. Using the speedboat in the Gather Data phase is best. Of course, you can use the same question that Hohmann posed, but I prefer a different question: "What's holding our team back from reaching full speed?" In this case, the anchors represent all the things that slow the team's work and that prevent it from finishing more quickly. This is a quick way to get some information that can, in the further stages of the retrospective, help you to find the experiment with the greatest potential. Determining the size of each anchor is also useful because you can then later focus your work on the biggest of them. The best tool for doing this is dot voting, which I already described in Chapter 1.

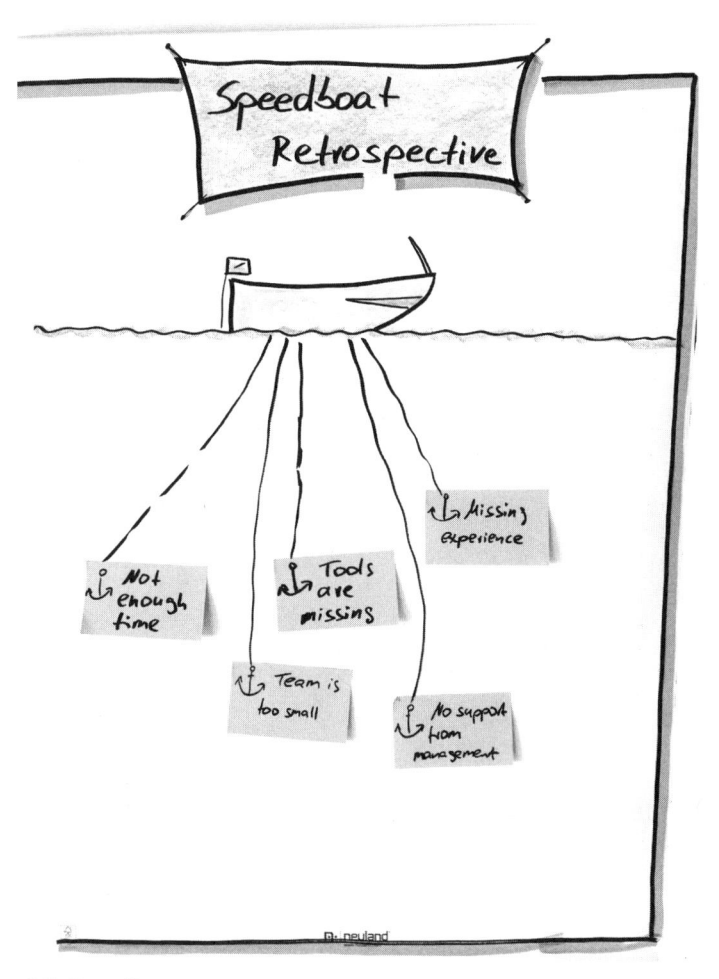

Figure 4-7 Speedboat retrospective

To extend this exercise, you can draw a cloud in one of the upper corners and ask the participants: "What are the gusts of the wind that help our sailboat to move forward?" Now we not only have anchors holding us back but the wind that blows to move us forward. This offers the possibility to turn each anchor into a gust of wind by following these three steps:

- Collect all the anchors, because collecting their current problems is easy to do for most teams.

- Ask the team to turn each anchor into goals, desires, or wishes, and put them before the cloud to represent the gusts of wind pushing the boat forward.
- Use these "winds" to define a desirable goal that you will use as true north for the rest of the retrospective.

The speedboat is a powerful metaphor that stimulates a lot of useful associations in the participants and thus leads to a good retrospective. You can also vary the metaphor: Use a race car (where the anchors are brake parachutes) or an airplane (where they're the baggage).

4.3.2 Trading Cards

Trading cards are everywhere! From *Star Wars* characters to wrestling stars of the WWF, innumerable kinds of these collectible, tradable cards exist. The parents of elementary school-aged children must be the worst afflicted, suffering, as they do, the trading card mania of their children. My sons like *Star Wars* trading cards at the moment (though they haven't seen any of the films). Most of these types of card have the following attributes:

- Name of the character or person
- Category of the card (for example, Jedi or Sith)
- Different strengths and weaknesses
- Sometimes also a saying or slogan that goes with the character

> **Practical Tip**
> Bring at least one example trading card to the retrospective. This makes it easier for the participants to understand what you want them to do.

In the Set the Stage phase, when a team is first formed and the members don't yet know each other very well, you can all create trading cards (see Figure 4-8) and swap them among you. Here's how it goes:

- Each participant gets a large note card and a marker.
- The participants get 5–10 minutes in which to create a trading card of themselves. This includes a self-portrait and a nickname. Additionally, each participant should write something on the card that he believes the others don't yet know about him.
- Now the cards are thoroughly traded by the participants until everyone has a card that he likes or finds particularly interesting.
- One after another, each team member reads the nickname on the card he ended up with and asks the person on the card something about the interesting detail included.

Figure 4-8 Example of a trading card

I personally enjoy this way of getting to know one another. It is a lot of fun, and there is also the potential to learn something new about your colleagues. This is also a comfortable way for people to introduce themselves because all the participants are doing so at the same time and not individually. This is a nice start, especially with new teams, and leads to a hopefully successful retrospective.

4.3.3 Perfection Game

The perfection game (see Figure 4-9) has nothing to do with its board game namesake from the 1980s. The perfection game described here is an aid for improving a given object that was developed by Steve de Shazer as part of his solution-oriented approach [4]. The technique was originally used to collect improvement suggestions for a wide range of things. I have used it many times, for example, to collect improvement suggestions for my presentations.

Before I give a presentation at a conference, I practice it in front of my colleagues. After the presentation, I put up a scale from 1–10 on a flipchart or whiteboard and ask the following question: "On a scale of 1–10, where one is very bad, and ten is very good, where would you put this presentation?" The participants answer this question by writing two things on a sticky note:

- What do you especially like about the presentation?
- What could I do differently to move my rating from x to x + 1 (for example, from 6 to 7)?

The participants then stick these sticky notes next to the scale. On the one hand, I get feedback about what is good about the presentation and on which I can continue to build, and, on the other, ideas on what and how to improve my presentation. I heartily recommend this technique to every presenter.

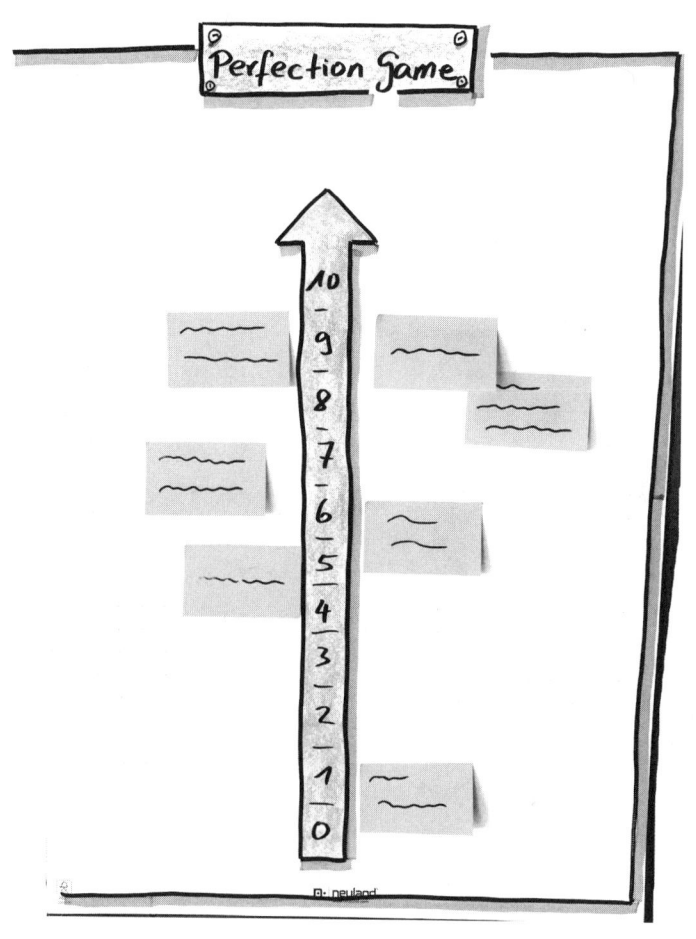

Figure 4-9 Perfection game

The perfection game is ideal for use at the end of a retrospective to define the next experiments. You show a scale from 1–10 on a flipchart or whiteboard. Now you ask the participants a question like "On a scale of 1–10, where one is very bad, and ten is very good, where would you put your current team performance?" The participants get sticky notes and answer the two questions:

- Where are we doing really well?
- What measures could we take to get our team performance from x to x + 1?

The results are a good impression of where the team sees itself and a collection of ideas for future experiments.

4.3.4 Force Field Analysis

Force field analysis (see Figure 4-10) is credited to the Gestalt psychologist Kurt Lewin and is used in the areas of social science, psychology, and process and change management [5]. The point of force field analysis is to show all the forces that either help or hinder a change. To start, you draw the potential change in the middle of a flipchart or whiteboard. On the left side, you write the heading "positive forces" and on the right, "negative forces." Then, you draw arrows from the left and right that point toward the middle.

> **Practical Tip**
> Make sure that the arrows are large enough that the group has enough room to label them.

After you have introduced the group to the topic, take the following steps:

1. Have each of the participants collect forces that positively support the possible change and write them on sticky notes.
2. Have them collect the forces that could obstruct the change.
3. Draw a simple scale from 1 to 5: One means the force is very weak, five means the force is very strong. Ask the participants to rate each of their forces according to the scale.
4. Put all the sticky notes up on an available bit of wall so that everyone can see them.
5. Have the participants work together to cluster their sticky notes and to name the resulting clusters.
6. Find an average rating for each cluster.

CHAPTER 4 • THE RETROSPECTIVE FACILITATOR

7. Transpose the cluster headings, together with their rating, to the force field analysis, either under "supporting forces" or "obstructing forces."

8. Find the total rating of each category and write this sum under the respective arrow. The result is a first impression of whether or not the potential change has a favorable outlook.

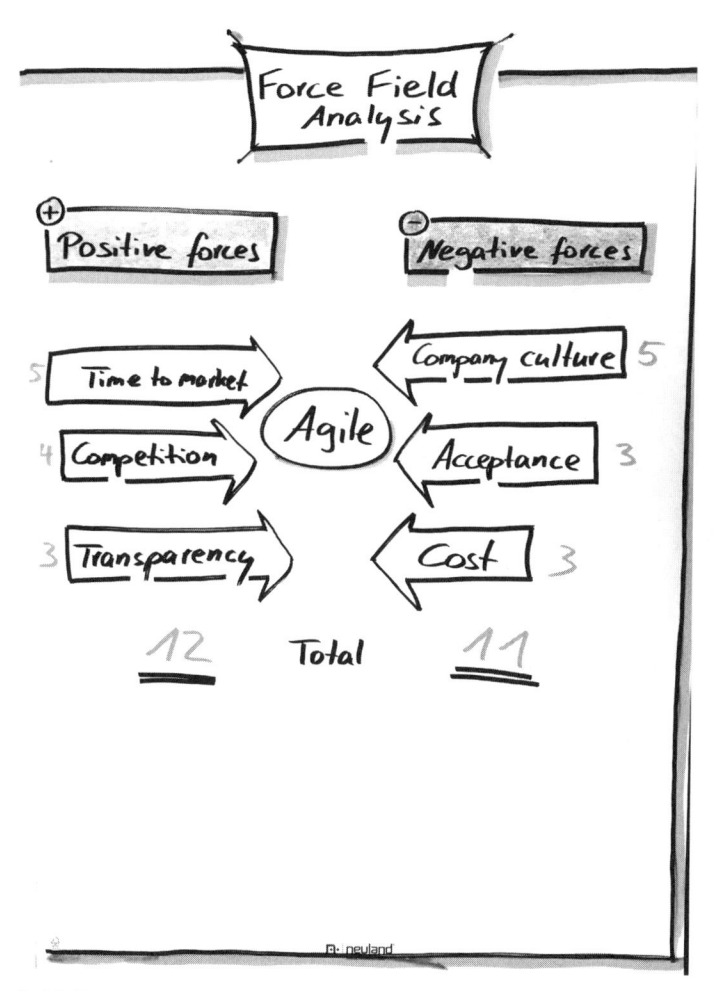

Figure 4-10 Force field analysis

Force field analysis can also be used outstandingly in retrospectives. You can use them at the end of a retrospective to judge the potential success of an experiment, or right at the beginning of a retrospective in the Gather Data phase. In this phase, there wouldn't be a potential change in the middle of the force field analysis, except, for example, a deliverable product. You would then collect all the forces that support getting a deliverable product as quickly as possible and all the forces that obstruct the team as they work. In the Generate Insights phase, you can analyze the forces, and later in the retrospective, you can define new experiments.

4.3.5 Sources of Inspiration for Visual Facilitation

It is more than obvious that the topic of visual facilitation cannot be covered comprehensively in this book; it's too large for that. Happily, a ton of literature is available to take you further on this topic and inspire you. The following books have all given me some helpful tips in the past and continue to help me today when I'm on the hunt for a new idea.

4.3.5.1 Visual Meetings

David Sibbet is one of the pre-eminent authorities on visual facilitation. He first developed techniques for accompanying workshops and meetings in the 1970s. In the 1980s he helped a number of companies to improve their work, including Apple. His book, *Visual Meetings* [6], is an outstanding introduction to the topic. From the very beginning, he goes into the advantages of visual work in any meeting and gives helpful tips on how to get better results on a whiteboard or flipchart. This book is a gold mine for people who are new to the topic, but experienced facilitators will certainly also be able to learn something new. This book belongs in every facilitation library.

4.3.5.2 The Graphic Facilitator's Guide

You might have seen a Graphic Facilitator covering the content of your last conference on a big sheet of paper. What these people are doing is outstanding. In her book, *The Graphic Facilitator's Guide* [7] Brandy Agerbeck covers all the important topics that you need to know about, to play such a role. But why am I listing this book here? As a retrospective's facilitator, you can benefit a lot from Brandy's book. It will help you to keep the group focused and productive, while you create organized and appealing flipcharts that point out patterns and make connections. As Brandy states, "Graphic facilitation is a powerful tool to help people feel heard, to develop a shared understanding as a group and be able to see and touch their work in a way they couldn't access before." These skills are more than helpful if you are facilitating a retrospective. In my opinion, this book also belongs on every facilitator's bookshelf.

4.3.5.3 *The Sketchnote Handbook*

The Sketchnote Handbook [8] is less about visually accompanying meetings and more about creating visual notes from meetings. In this book, Mike Rhode takes you step by step through visual notes. I've included it in this list for two reasons. First, at the beginning of the book, he gives some drawing tips that can be used anywhere. Second, I find this technique very valuable when it comes to recording the results of a retrospective in a visual format. The book is also illustrated all the way through and is a lot of fun to read. Many of the tips for the structure of visual notes can be carried over one to one to the structure of flipcharts or whiteboards. It can also help you if you have always been frustrated when it comes to creating notes from a presentation. This book isn't a must in a facilitation library but has definitely earned a place.

4.4 Internal or External

When you are looking for a facilitator for a retrospective, you must ask yourself whether he should come from within the team (internal) or from outside it (external). Both have their advantages and disadvantages, but in general, an external facilitator is usually the better choice. There are several reasons for this.

The first and most important reason is that a facilitator who is not part of the team is, in most cases, neutral. He has no preconceived opinion and can, therefore, moderate the retrospective in a more neutral way. An internal facilitator can have difficulty maintaining this neutrality because he is a part of the team and often has his own opinion on particular topics. The inherent danger is that a discussion could develop one-sidedly, which could prevent the team from finding the best possible solution. Emotions, too, play a role, in that they can negatively affect a retrospective: whether it's because of personal differences or because the decisions made affect the facilitator's own area of work. A neutral facilitator has no personal point of view and can make sure that everyone has an opportunity to speak and that a common consensus is reached. This is the only way for a facilitator to support a team as well as possible.

The desire to play two roles during a retrospective can become a problem for internal facilitators. On one hand, they are team members and want to, or must, actively contribute to the retrospective. On the other, they are facilitators and should thus moderate the retrospective and support the team in its work. To hold both roles is extremely difficult, principally because of having to switch constantly between them. For one who is new to the role of facilitator, the switching is even more difficult. An external facilitator doesn't have this problem. He can concentrate fully on his role and support the team. He is 100% facilitator and there for the team.

Sometimes a situation is so muddled that calling in a professional for the retrospective makes sense. This should be a person with a great deal of experience as a facilitator of workshops in general and retrospectives in particular. What you get is a neutral facilitator who can help a group through difficult conditions, understands group dynamics, and can clarify confusing situations. You can also learn a lot from this kind of person. The internal facilitator could potentially lead the retrospective alongside the external facilitator, thus increasing his learning.

A further reason for hiring someone from outside can be that there simply isn't anyone internal either willing or able to take on the role of facilitator. In this case, there's no way around looking for an external facilitator.

In writing here about external facilitators, I don't necessarily mean someone from outside your company. Experienced facilitators who can help in these situations are often within a company. What do you do, though, if you can't find an external facilitator and you always have an internal facilitator?

4.4.1 Tips for Internal Facilitators

Sometimes you have no option but to appoint an internal facilitator. Different reasons for this can include:

- The company doesn't want to pay for external facilitators.
- You're the first team that is carrying out retrospectives.
- You want to moderate your own retrospectives.

In many Scrum teams, the facilitator is the Scrum Master. In other teams, it might perhaps be the person who most enjoys running workshops. If you're an internal facilitator, you have to be aware of the problems described earlier and learn to live with them.

As to the question of neutrality, don't kid yourself: If you are a part of the team, staying neutral is very difficult. Try anyway. You'll only be accepted as the facilitator when the other team members see that you are interested in making sure that all opinions are heard. Take special care that all the participants have the opportunity to express their opinions. At the same time, you have to make sure that all relevant topics are discussed and that each one is apportioned sufficient time. You can use a few techniques to help you do this well.

4.4.1.1 Role Change

An internal facilitator always has the problem of feeling the need to take on two roles during a retrospective.

- The role of the facilitator
- The role of team member and participant

This is not at all easy and should be avoided if possible.

> **Practical Tip**
> Really try to avoid this role swap. If you're the facilitator of the retrospective, then stay in that role. Otherwise, being a good facilitator is difficult.

Switching between roles makes things difficult, not only for you but also for the other participants, for whom it will not always be clear which role you are in at any given moment during the retrospective. If you cannot avoid this double role, you can do two things that have proved helpful in the past.

The first is to make it clear which role you are currently holding. One way to do that is with verbal announcements like, for example, "I'm now slipping into the role of facilitator again." Or, "Now I'm part of the team again." Another way that has also proven to be good practice is to mark your current role visually. For example, stick a big sticky note on the whiteboard that names your current role. The best thing is to have sticky notes of different colors; then the difference is even more clearly portrayed. When you change the notes, you make the role change visible to everyone. Of course, you can also stick the note on your chest. Some teams have different hats, which represent the different roles. So, for example, a hard hat for when you're a team member and a pilot's cap for when you've picked up the role of facilitator again. There are no limits to your imagination here. However, if you do it, make sure that all the team members, as well as yourself, of course, know what role you are in at any point.

The second is to rotate the role of a facilitator from retrospective to retrospective; each team member takes a turn leading a retrospective. This way, you avoid the need to take on both roles during a retrospective. If you rotate the role, then whichever team member is the facilitator can concentrate on it fully, because in the next retrospective he'll be a team member again. Using this method spares you a lot of schizophrenia. An additional advantage of this model is that, because of the rotation, you get more variety in the retrospectives. Everyone has his particular way of leading a retrospective and different ideas about what activities to use. Rotation can also be helpful when no one wants to take on the role of facilitator.

4.4.2 External Facilitators

The advantages of external facilitators have already been described. They are neutral, can concentrate on the role of facilitator, and might well have more experience. But external facilitators need not strictly mean facilitators from outside a particular company. There are often several teams in a company carrying out retrospectives, and this allows for the opportunity of "borrowing" a facilitator from another team. A good practice is for two teams to agree to exchange team members for leading each other's retrospectives. The advantages are clear:

- You don't need to spend money on an external facilitator—a big expenditure in many companies.
- The facilitator from another team brings all the advantages of an external facilitator.
- The agreement between the teams means that you always have an external facilitator at hand.
- You don't experience the problem of having to switch between different roles.

Sometimes, though, calling in an experienced facilitator from outside the company can make sense. This might be for one of the following reasons:

- You are new to facilitation and want to experience how a retrospective is lead by an external facilitator. You could also get the external facilitator to include a workshop on leading retrospectives.
- You are at the end of a longer project phase and want to carry out a half- or whole-day retrospective.
- You want to carry out a very large retrospective with several teams. In this situation, having more than one facilitator can be an advantage.
- You are in a muddled situation that involves not only the team but also the whole system; in other words, the whole company. Here, you can profit from both the facilitator's neutrality, as well as his outside eye on the system.

Experience has shown that, in practice, you should only appoint external facilitators periodically. Training internal team members and thus increasing the knowledge-base in the company makes more sense. It is cheaper in the long run and, it helps change the culture of a company gradually. Retrospectives have the biggest effect in cultures that really live continuous improvement.

> **Practical Tip**
> If you call an external facilitator into the company, lead the retrospective with him. That way, you learn more and can use what you learn in your future retrospectives.

4.5 After the Retro Is Before the Retro

As Sepp Herberger said so nicely: "After the game is before the game." That's exactly how it is with retrospectives. If you take the process of continuous improvement seriously, you must repeat retrospectives at regular intervals. However, starting from scratch every time doesn't make any sense. Ideally, individual retrospectives are interconnected and thus make possible a goal-oriented process. To be able to do that, though, you have to invest time in evaluating the retrospective. By doing this, you ensure both that the results are not lost and that they are actually worked through.

The evaluation of every workshop, and especially retrospectives, is one of the most important tasks of a facilitator. All the results that were worked out during the retrospective have to be documented. I don't mean long and wordy minutes, but so-called "photo minutes," or photographic documentation of the retrospective. This involves photographing all the elements of a retrospective, beginning with the agenda and going all the way up to the experiments that were agreed upon, as well as their hypotheses. The photos, with no comments attached, go into a common document. This can be a PowerPoint presentation, a word document or simply a wiki page. This document is then shared with all the participants, with emphasis on the finished experiments. But that's not all. Not for nothing do we say "out of sight, out of mind." The problem with these documents is that they are only seldom looked at a second or third time. That is why it is extremely important that the actual decisions are visible to the team at all times. Only then can you make sure that they are actually worked through.

Some teams hang their photo documentation in the most prominent place in the whole company: by the coffee machine. Doing this makes sure that the results of your meetings are visible to all. If that doesn't work for you, then you must at least make sure that the results are hanging up in the team room. Results mean, for a retrospective, the experiments to be carried out, along with their hypotheses.

Unfortunately, people become accustomed to things hanging up very quickly and, with time, come to ignore them. That's why moving the results and hanging them somewhere else now and then is a good idea.

> **Practical Tip**
> If the team works with a task board, that is, a whiteboard that depicts all the tasks on which a team is currently working (in Scrum that would be the sprint backlog, in Kanban the Kanban board), then display the tasks from the retrospective there. In most cases, a team meets in front of a board like this once a day and thus has the opportunity of planning the experiments into their daily running. At the same time, the status of the experiment is made visible, so that everyone knows if an experiment is already being worked on, if it hasn't been started, or if it's already done.

The displayed results will be removed from the board and taken into the next retrospective when it takes place (of course, you should note the status of the experiments). Doing this makes sure that you follow up the results of the experiments and creates the basis for new experiments.

Summary

In this chapter, you got all the basics that you need to become a great retrospective facilitator. We started with some facilitation tools such as paraphrasing, stacking, or intended silence that you can immediately use in your next retrospective. Additionally, you learned about all the important stuff to create eye-catching visuals and saw some examples.

I also covered the pros and cons of internal and external facilitators and reminded you that the next retrospective is always coming up.

Now that you have learned the basics, it is time to take a deep dive into the more advanced topics. See you there.

References

[1] Julian Treasure. "5 ways to listen better." https://www.ted.com/talks/julian_treasure_5_ways_to_listen_better.

[2] Sam Kaner. 2014. *Facilitator's Guide to Participatory Decision-Making*. Jossey-Bass.

[3] Luke Hohmann. 2006. *Innovation Games: Creating Breakthrough Products Through Collaborative Play*. Addison-Wesley Professional.

[4] Steve de Shazer. https://en.wikipedia.org/wiki/Steve_de_Shazer.

[5] Force-field Analysis. https://en.wikipedia.org/wiki/Force-field_analysis.

[6] David Sibbet. 2010. *Visual Meetings: How Graphics, Sticky Notes and Idea Mapping Can Transform Group Productivity*. Wiley.

[7] Brandy Agerbeck. 2012. *The Graphic Facilitator's Guide: How to Use Your Listening, Thinking and Drawing Skills to Make Meaning*. Loosetooth.com Library.

[8] Mike Rhode. 2012. *The Sketchnote Handbook: The Illustrated Guide to Visual Note Taking*. Peachpit Press.

5

From the Metaphor to the Retrospective

After facilitating some retrospectives, you'll find that you have hit a wall in your efforts to keep them varied. If you're always wanting to try something new, there simply aren't enough good ideas for fresh retrospectives. There's nothing for it then, but to come up with some activities of your own.

Using theme-based metaphors is a very effective method for "inventing" new ways to lead retrospectives. You can draw these themes from practically everything: from cars to xylophones. The best themes are those that you, or someone around you, knows well. After you've decided on a theme, you can start to come up with activities relevant to the theme's context. The first step is to make a list of all the terms that occur to you in connection with the chosen theme. In most cases, this is quite quick and simple, and though it might sometimes take a bit longer to find the right terms, it is a lot of fun. There are two advantages to doing this as a group: First, you get more ideas. Second, it's more fun.

When you've created the list of terms, you can begin to come up with some relevant activities. You must always keep in mind what you want to achieve in the particular phases of the retrospective and choose appropriate metaphors from the context of the chosen theme. For example, in looking for an appropriate metaphor for the Gather Data phase, you have to make sure that the resulting activity will help you achieve your goals for that phase. Here is an illustration: Let's say that you've chosen the theme "travel." An ideal activity from this theme for the Gather Data phase is a travelogue. In this case, the team would write a travelogue or travel report for the period under consideration.

An important part of your job as the facilitator is ensuring that, during discussions, the team only use terms from the chosen theme. This is advantageous because it allows the team to put some distance between itself and the events that actually occurred. In my experience, team members find it significantly easier to discuss awkward subjects when they can use a metaphor to do so. Using metaphors from the theme loosens up the atmosphere of a retrospective and can even be a lot of fun. For example, talking about "dirty tackles" and "dives" in a football retrospective is much easier than it might otherwise be to bring up and discuss the events they represent in everyday office language.

> **Practical Tip**
>
> My mother was once so completely fed up with having to decide on the family meal every day that she instituted a four-week dinner schedule. Every four weeks, the cycle began again. Rump steak every day would be boring, but if you only have it once every couple of weeks, it keeps its appeal. The same idea can be applied to retrospectives.
>
> Having to come up with a brand-new retrospective every 2–4 weeks would get pretty draining. Instead, develop a schedule that alternates theme-based retrospectives with "normal" ones. The schedule might look like this (I explain all the metaphor examples listed in the course of this chapter):
>
> - Football retrospective
> - Standard retrospective
> - Orchestra retrospective

> - Standard retrospective
> - Train retrospective
> - Standard retrospective
>
> Of course, you needn't pull a new theme-based retrospective out of your hat every second time; you can also repeat them.

The rest of this chapter consists of suggestions for theme-based retrospective activities, with possible activities discussed phase by phase.

> **Practical Tip**
>
> As the "Check Hypotheses" phase requires no special activities, I have not included it in the examples that follow. However, you should not skip this phase in your own retrospectives and should always check your hypotheses from the last retrospective.

Let's say that you decide on an orchestra theme.

5.1 The Orchestra Retrospective

To get into the theme, let's have a brief look at the work of an orchestra. That's easy for me, as I play the saxophone in an orchestra. A typical year for us looks something like this:

At the beginning of the year, our first appearance is the New Year's Reception in the town hall. At the end of January, we have our annual general meeting. At Shrovetide (Fasching or Fastnacht), we play at different parades. In spring, we have the first highlight: the spring concert. Between spring and summer, we play in various concerts, from morning pints to gala concerts. In the summer, we then have a six-week break, in which there are no concerts or rehearsals.

After the summer break, we start intensive rehearsals for the next highlight: the autumn concert. After the autumn concert, we play another one or two; our double concerts with other societies are often during this period. Then comes Christmas, when we occasionally play at local Christmas markets. Over the Christmas holidays, we have a short break in rehearsals before it all kicks off again in January. Of course, throughout the year we also accompany the typical Martinmas parades, communions, and other holidays.

When you've become sufficiently familiar with your topic, you can begin to define the particular phases of the retrospective. Let's have a go.

5.1.1 Set the Stage

When using a theme in the Set the Stage phase, putting together a list of terms relevant to your chosen theme is a good practice. After a short introduction, you and the participants create this list together at the beginning of the phase. The mere writing of this list helps the participants to immerse themselves into the world of the theme. The list for the orchestra retrospective could look something like this:

- Musicians
- Conductor
- Conductor's baton
- Section
- Sheet Music
- Music Stands
- Instruments
- Music
- Instrument Stands / Microphone
- Uniform
- Solo

- Soloist
- Unison
- Cluster
- Time
- Bar
- Volume
- Song/Singing

Only these terms will be used in the rest of the retrospective.

> **Practical Tip**
>
> The facilitator's task is to make sure that only the collected terms are used over the course of the retrospective. The best thing to do is write the list on a sheet of flipchart paper and hang it up in the room so that it is clearly visible. These terms will often generate associations to actual events.

5.1.2 Gather Data

Data-gathering is, above all, about creating a full picture and common understanding. How might an orchestra do this?

At the beginning of the year, most orchestral societies have their annual general meeting (AGM). Part of the AGM is the secretary's report. This report summarizes almost all the events, the concerts, and often the amusing occurrences of the last year and is thus a retrospective of that year. You do exactly the same in your retrospective. However, instead of having just one secretary, the whole team acts as secretary. So, you ask team members to place themselves in the role of the secretary and to present the desired period of time as an annual report.

This report is best represented as a timeline, which naturally comprises a whole year. Each participant gets a marker and some sticky notes and writes down the events from the period that are particularly memorable. He then adds these events to the timeline. Additionally, each person represents his personal mood during the period by drawing a line with all the emotional up and downs below the timeline.

As the facilitator, you must make sure that the team members stick with the orchestra metaphor and use the orchestra vocabulary. The advantage of this approach is that many people find it easier to describe things pictorially rather than to address them directly. At the same time, it is a lot of fun and loosens the atmosphere, which later makes it easier to discuss awkward topics. As a facilitator, seeing how the participants gradually fill in the timeline with their events is especially exciting.

> **Practical Tip**
>
> As the facilitator, keep reminding the participants of the theme being used and ask them relevant questions. For example:
>
> - What made you mad about your conductor last year?
> - Which concert trips do you remember particularly well?
> - Where there problems with playing together?
> - Are you satisfied with your instruments?
> - What bothered you about your sheet music?
> - Which solo did you like best last year?
>
> With these questions, you can help the team members to keep their heads in the world of the orchestra. Additionally, it helps them to recall the events of the period in question.

At the end of this phase, you give the "members of the orchestra" time to go through the annual report. Only after this should any questions be answered or any concerns discussed in detail. Armed with this annual report, you then move into the next phase.

5.1.3 Generate Insights

Of course, as for every orchestra, not everything will have run smoothly for you. But there must have been some positive things, or even surprises, that no one had anticipated. Because you can't discuss everything, the "orchestra" must settle on only a few things before you can move forward with the phase. The best way to choose these discussion topics is to use the dot voting method (refer to Chapter 1, "Retrospectives 101"). Members can stick the dots on any event they like. How many to stick up per event is up to each person.

> **Practical Tip**
> As the facilitator, emphasize that the participants can also stick their dots on positive events. Working further on these topics so as to steadily improve them can often be valuable. It is important that a retrospective not focus solely on negatives.

In this way, the team has, in the end, chosen a maximum of three topics on which it wants to work over the course of the retrospective. Now it's time to generate insights on these topics. There are many ways to do this, but how might an orchestra generate insights?

When an orchestra is rehearsing a new piece, it often gets stuck in a few places. To get to the bottom of this, the conductor often has a single section play alone (for example, just the trombones, or just the violins), instead of having the whole orchestra play together. This helps the conductor find the root of the current problem. So, take on the role of the conductor and ask yourself:

- How does this problem sound in a certain section of my orchestra (that is, the test section)?
- Why did a certain section play that part particularly well?
- Why is section X unable to master a particular part?

Collect answers to these questions. Discuss the results. Generate insights. When you look at a problem from a completely different point of view (the point of view of an orchestra), you suddenly come to new insights. This phase is best carried out in small groups of 3–5 people. Discussions like these are hard to carry out in groups any larger than this. At the end of this phase, each group presents the insights it generated. Of course, questions from the other groups are allowed. The results that teams get when they work with themes are always surprising. After all the insights have been shared, it's time to move on to the next phase.

5.1.4 Define Experiments and Hypothesis

Now that you know, or think you know, why one section plays a part so outstandingly well, or another breaks down at the same spot, it's time to try out something new. You once more take on the role of the conductor.

In an orchestra, there is a lot of experimentation. Our conductor often gives us instructions such as, "Try to play this part like…," or "Could you try playing a bit louder from bar 57 on?" or "Have a go at letting the staccato ring a little." In the end, all of these instructions are nothing but experiments. The advantage of an orchestra is that the resulting hypotheses can be tested very quickly. As a conductor, you know within half a minute whether you've gotten the desired effect and can adapt your experiment, if necessary.

Take on the role of the conductor once again and ask yourself the following questions:

- How can I help section X to master the part better?
- What load can I take off another section?
- How can I play the part even better?
- Where do I need to develop my orchestra further?
- Where can musicians from other sections support an undermanned section?

By getting the answers to these questions, you get a list of possible experiments for the next iteration; for example, to move the solo from one section to another or to do a section rehearsal. It goes without saying that you can't try all the experiments at once. For one, you wouldn't know which experiment was responsible for the final result and, for another, many changes at one time often lead to complications.

Again, the dot voting can help you to choose the most promising experiments. After you've agreed on a maximum of two experiments, you have to define the respective hypotheses, because, without hypotheses, retrospectives seldom lead to accomplishing goals. The most important thing is to make sure that the hypotheses can be tested. The only good hypothesis is a one that can be tested. Armed with new ideas for the next iteration, you now bid the team a suitable farewell.

5.1.5 Closing

The experiments and hypotheses have been defined, now the next steps can be briefly summarized. When it is clear how the experiments should be carried out, it is time for a powerful closing. The team's hard work should be suitably celebrated and what's better than a good piece of music to kick off the next iteration with a load of energy?

How about Handel's "Music for the Royal Fireworks," for example? If that's too classical for you, I'm sure you can find something to your taste, such as *We Will Rock You* by Queen. In any event, you should close this retrospective with an energetic piece of music. You can be sure that no one's going to forget this retrospective in a hurry.

5.2 The Soccer Retrospective

In the spring of 2012, a company asked me to lead a retrospective for them. I agreed at once. It was clear to me from the beginning that I didn't want to give them an everyday retrospective. So, I had a think about what theme might go down well. As the UEFA Euro 2012 was just around the corner, I had the idea of doing a soccer retrospective. The people hiring me were enthusiastic about the idea, so I sat down and came up with some activities I could use in the particular phases of the retrospective.

5.2.1 Preparation

So that a theme-based retrospective will bear fruit, decorating the room appropriately is helpful. In the case of the soccer retrospective, you naturally want to get the team into a soccer mood. So, you take a few soccer balls, a few jerseys, Panini collectible stickers, and other soccer fan accessories and prepare the room. If you don't have the opportunity to get these things, the least you can do is draw a soccer pitch on a piece of flipchart paper. Apart from that, you require the usual suspects:

- Felt markers
- Flipchart paper
- Sticky notes
- Something to get your teeth into

5.2.2 Set the Stage

To bring everyone into the soccer mood and to clarify the terms, you have a small brainstorming round in the Set the Stage phase. The goal of the brainstorming is to collect as many soccer terms as possible and write them on a piece of flipchart paper. Hang the results up in the room so they are clearly visible for the rest of the retrospective. This is a good cheat sheet for the next phases and later helps you to find good soccer metaphors for the events of the past days and weeks. A possible list might look like this:

- Goal
- Fouls
- Yellow/Red Card

- Counterattack
- Substitution
- Line-up
- Tactics
- Penalty Spot
- Referee
- Striker
- Defender
- Coach
- Ball
- Touchline

5.2.3 *Gather Data*

The first step in the Gather Data phase is to review the last "game." To do that, form groups with a maximum of five people and have them reconstruct the "Live Ticker," the live online ticker that summarizes the minute-by-minute events of a match—when the goals were scored; who was fouled by whom; when there were substitutions, penalties, exciting counterattacks; and so on. The groups transpose their last iteration into the 90 minutes of a soccer match (with the option of adding injury time and penalties) and collect all the events that occurred during their "match." Use the soccer terms that you collected in the previous stage to help with this phase.

> **Practical Tip**
>
> Give the participants a few examples such as, "We had two late goals in the 88th and 89th minute" or "We had to play with only nine players from the 67th minute because the rest were taken out of the game." There are no limits to creativity here.

In my experience, teams have a lot of fun with this. The first laughs are sure to come, at the latest, when "dirty tackles" come into the discussion. The result of the work in this phase is a live ticker listing individual moments of the match and the events that occurred in them.

To build a common picture, each team now presents its match and the events it has listed. Then comes the game analysis, because, after all, you want to get a better result in the next match.

5.2.4 Generating Insights

Without a detailed match analysis, working out meaningful changes for the next match is hard. That is why the individual groups should now take on the role of head coach and analyze the events of the last match. Again, as the facilitator, try to get the team to stick to the soccer theme. It is up to the groups whether to use techniques like "the 5-Why method" or a fishbone diagram for the analysis. After the individual group analysis, the groups come together and share what they've learned. You might hear insights such as, "At the substitution, we got handball players instead of soccer players" or "the referee wasn't really present" or "instead of working as a team, everyone just played for himself" or "we have too many strikers." Now you have a good foundation for developing new tactics, changes to the team, and more.

5.2.5 Define Next Experiments and Hypothesis

Now it's time to plan experiments for the next match. The group is now the coaching staff of the team and has to consider, on the basis of the preceding analysis, what needs to change regarding tactics, training, lineup, and so on. How can they prevent the mistakes and problems of the last match from happening again in the next one? How can they play an even better match? In the end, the groups present their results. Make sure that the team doesn't take on too much;

less is more. Furthermore, you need to make sure that someone from the coaching team is responsible for each measure. Of course, the hypothesis is extremely important, so for each measure, the team must define a hypothesis that can be tested and followed up on in the next retrospective.

5.2.6 Closing

The next match is imminent. Like every team just before kickoff, everyone gets into a circle, and the captain of the team says a few inspiring words. Then there is a short battle cry, and the team can plunge into the next iteration.

5.3 The Train Retrospective

The train retrospective and the upcoming kitchen retrospective theme are the result of an open space session that I led at the Agile Coaching Camp Germany 2013. Thanks to all the participants for that session and for allowing me to use the results here.

In the train retrospective example, the idea is to see the time period being worked on as a train journey.

5.3.1 Set the Stage

As in the other theme-based retrospectives, having the participants collect relevant terms and write them on a piece of flipchart paper makes sense. As a group of four at the Coach Camp, we got 41 terms in 5 minutes, despite the fact that one of the participants was worried that the topic wouldn't yield enough. Here is a small excerpt from that list:

- Conductor
- Ticket
- Tunnel

- Bridge
- Derailment
- Compartment
- Passenger
- Restaurant Car
- Station

When we made that list, I discovered once again just how easily these terms come to mind. This topic seems to be one with which one can identify easily and quickly.

5.3.2 Gather Data

As always, this phase is about calling to mind the last weeks, or perhaps months. Because the theme of the retrospective is *train*, what would be more fitting than to collect those events in the form of an account of the train journey? The idea is to describe the journey from the last retrospective to today, or from point A to point B. Naturally, you will again use the terms that you collected in the first phase.

When I think about my last train journey, I can recall an awful lot that I could use as metaphors to depict events in a retrospective. In thinking about some of your own journeys, you'll realize the same: There was the delayed train, which resulted in missing a connecting train; the excessively large suitcase that you nearly couldn't get down the narrow aisle; the class of school children that made a lot noise, and so on. Many things also happen in a railway station that can be ideal metaphors for describing your events: the homeless man begging for money; learning too late that you're on the wrong platform; the friend you coincidentally meet; the vending machine that won't take your money.

You can easily see that metaphors from this theme have a great potential to help with the description of the events occurred. Let's say that Peter was taken from the team during the last iteration and given other tasks. With the help of a metaphor, you could describe it like this: "Peter got off the train two stations early and thus could take no further part in the train journey. Instead, he got on a different train with a new destination." Or, let's say that the team couldn't carry out any of the tasks it had agreed on. With another metaphor from our theme, you could describe it like this: "Our train was left standing in the middle of a stretch of track and had to be towed by another train." If there were communication problems because different parties work in completely different places, you could describe it like this: "A part of our team sat in a completely different compartment or even carriage."

Let's go back to the example metaphors I gave earlier. What could be represented with the metaphor of a loud class of school children? This might, for example, be a loud, open-plan office. The large suitcase is perhaps the new feature that was too big to implement. The missed train might be a missed opportunity. You can see the possibilities are many and varied.

> **Practical Tip**
>
> Even though my examples are almost all negative (perhaps I've just had too many negative experiences on trains), you should make sure that there are some positive results. Too many negative results and you run the risk of a negative retrospective.

To write the travel report, divide the participants into groups of a maximum of four people, who then present their reports. Before you climb onto the next phase, you decide, as a team, which events you will work on over the rest of the retrospective.

5.3.3 Generate Insights

Often, we take photos on our journeys so as to have lovely mementos of the days we spent together. We can fondly remember our journeys with the help of these photos, but we can also use them to reconstruct events.

Normally, of course, you don't have any photos of the events of a project. If you do happen to have any, bring them with you to the retrospective. The idea of this phase is to analyze the events by using a photo gallery to trace a line through them. Again, you form small groups, each with a maximum of four people. Each group gets paper and markers to tell the story of an event. It is best to start in the present and go back into the past, step by step. You can use the 5-Why method to make this process easier. Thus, you gradually get a kind of comic strip that tells the story of the team and that, in the end, allows you to see the results that are to be analyzed. As in the other phases, make sure to stick to the theme of a train journey and only use the relevant terms.

In the end, each group presents its photo gallery. If two groups have worked on the same topic, they present together. The analyzed photo galleries are the foundation for the next phase, the planning of the next train ride.

5.3.4 Define Experiments and Hypothesis

Now it's time to continue the train journey. To do this, you have to establish mutually how you want to structure the next segment of the journey. So you make a travel plan. Again, you form small groups of a maximum of four participants. The task of each group is now to create a travel plan that includes the following elements:

- Where do we want to go?
- What did we forget last time and want to take with us this time?
- What things do we want to keep?
- What should we definitely avoid this time?
- Optional: a travel checklist for each participant.

By generating a travel plan, you get lists of ideas for the next train ride from all the groups. To consolidate the lists, you all agree on the one or two things with the largest apparent potential.

In closing, you have to translate the results. After all, not everyone's going to take to the idea of traveling with smaller suitcases. Instead, you establish, for example, that you will try to produce smaller work packages in the next project phase. In all the fun, you should also remember to make sure that the results are actionable (SMART—see Chapter 3, "The First Retrospective") and to define a fitting hypothesis. When you've taken care of that, then you're ready for the next stage of the journey.

5.3.5 *Closing*

As has been so nicely expressed about soccer: After the game is before the game. Of course, the same goes for the train journey: After the leg of the journey is before the leg of the journey. In the closing round, briefly review what you have decided on and who is responsible for enacting the particular aspects of the journey that you have planned. At the very end, you all meet on an imaginary platform (at the exit to the room) and get on the train to begin the next phase of the journey (you leave the room and go back to work).

5.4 The Kitchen Retrospective

As I mentioned earlier, the kitchen retrospective also came out of the Agile Coach Camp 2013. The team first worked on a computer retrospective, but then turned away and disappeared, figuratively speaking, into the kitchen. As we subsequently discovered, you can get great metaphors out of this theme.

5.4.1 *Set the Stage*

As with the other theme-based retrospectives, you start the kitchen retrospective by collecting terms associated with the kitchen. These can be kitchen appliances or utensils, ingredients, or even recipes. Here is a small sample list:

- Wooden spoon
- Pan
- Exhaust fan

- Stove top
- Oven
- Pepper
- Salt
- Knife
- Serving fork
- Saucepan

Even as I was making this list, I thought of lots of ways to use these terms over the course of a retrospective. I especially like the exhaust fan.

5.4.2 Gather Data

The idea of the kitchen retrospective is to assess the current state of the kitchen. What is or was in the fridge? Is there or was there a shopping list? If yes, what's on it? What does the kitchen situation look like? How have the last dishes left the kitchen? Were they burnt or oversalted? Was there enough on the plate? Was there enough for everyone to eat? Do you have everything you need? What does the appliance situation look like? Do the appliances function as desired? Is there enough stock for the upcoming period? What needs to be bought? Are you any good at the recipes? Are there too many cooks in the kitchen? The answers to these questions go, as always, on sticky notes that are then put on a large piece of empty wall.

> **Practical Tip**
> Make sure that each sticky note has only one answer to it. Otherwise grouping them later is hard.

At this point you can, if it's possible, group the sticky notes by topic. To rate the different topics, you could use my beloved dot voting method.

You can see how wonderfully such a kitchen can help a team, project, or company to address the most varied things. Despite the fact that the kitchen is a very small room, compared to a train at least, it holds many metaphors with which you can experiment when gathering data. The best thing to do would simply be to try it out in your next retrospective.

5.4.3 Generate Insights

The current condition of the kitchen can be fairly shattering. That is why it is now your task to find out what has caused this condition. To do this, you concentrate on the topics you selected using dot voting. Implement the 5-Why question technique or use a fishbone diagram to help you get to the bottom of things. Another possibility would be to ask the customers.

> **What Is a Fishbone Diagram?**
>
> The fishbone diagram (see Figure 5-1) is described in *Agile Retrospectives: Making Good Teams Great* by Esther Derby and Diana Larsen [1, p. 87] and is a method for identifying the main causes of problems. Some of you may know it as an Ishikawa diagram [2]. First, you draw the scaffold, the fish bones. You write in the problem itself near the fish's head. The individual bones are divided into categories: methods, materials, people, rules, surroundings, suppliers, skills, and so on. Then you start brainstorming. You look for factors in each of the categories that either cause or affect the problem. These factors are either written directly onto the "bones," or you can use sticky notes. Of each factor, you then ask the question, "why?" You keep doing that until the causes you find lie outside the team's area of influence. Now you look for factors that appear in more than one category. These are the causes with the greatest potential for improvement and which thus become your focus for the rest of the retrospective.

Figure 5-1 Example of a fishbone diagram

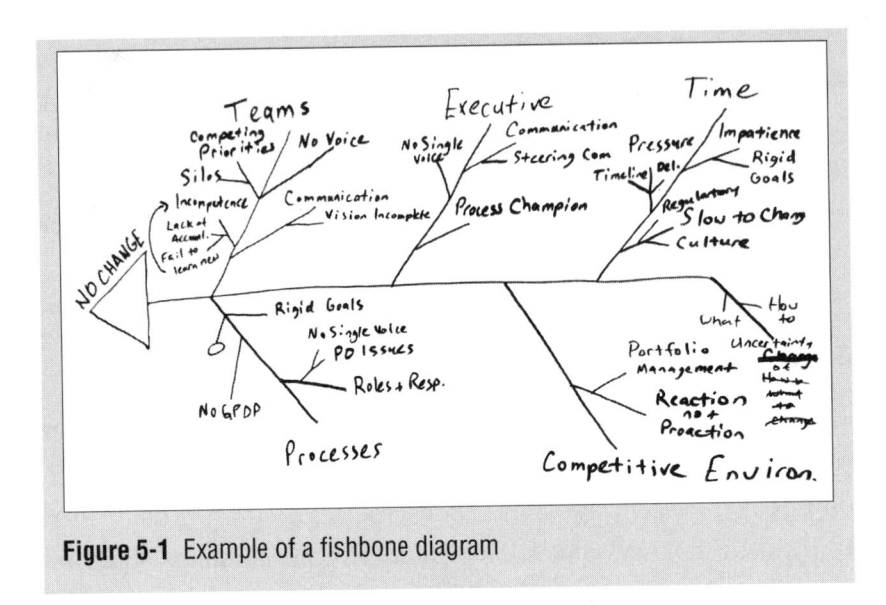

If you think of the kitchen, not as a kitchen in your own home, but as a large kitchen in a restaurant, then, of course, there are always the customers. You can consult the customers in different ways. When only the internal team is present, you split the team into kitchen staff and customers.

> **Practical Tip**
> If people from outside the team take part as actual internal or external customers, then this group of people forms the customer group.

You then form groups of 4–6 people, of which half are customers and half kitchen staff. If not enough customers are present, then you must adapt the grouping accordingly. Now it's time to consult the customers. Here the kitchen staff confines itself to the previously selected topic areas. Some questions could be, "Why didn't you like dish x?" or "What was missing in your opinion?" Here again, you make sure always to stay in the context of the kitchen by using the kitchen terminology. With the resulting stock of insights, you can then start on the next phase.

5.4.4 Define Experiments and Hypothesis

The customers have gone, and you've almost come to the end of the retrospective. Like any good cook, you want to cook even better for your customers tomorrow and serve them up some creative dishes. That is why you now get together and consider how to improve the kitchen and how to rework some details of the recipes. To do that, you answer the following questions:

- What experiment can we do to improve our kitchen?
- How can we shorten the time between the customer's order and our delivery of the cooked dish?
- Which of our recipes is in need of an overhaul, and what should we try to improve?

Of course, you can't change everything all at once, because then you can't be sure which experiments gave which results. You must, therefore, decide on one or two experiments and define hypotheses for these accordingly. When you've done that, it's time for the closing.

5.4.5 Closing

Why shouldn't you end a retrospective with a tasty dessert? This will strengthen you for the next project phase and will give you the chance to review the next steps once more while you eat.

5.5 The Pirate Retrospective

I had the idea for a retrospective based on a pirate theme at the ALE Conference (Agile Lean Europe) in Barcelona, in September 2012. There I met Gitte Klitgaard Hansen, who is a big fan of pirates. During the conference, I suggested an open space session to generate new theme-based retrospective activities. One of the themes was pirates. Unfortunately, at the time we were completely out of ideas and couldn't come up with any activities for this theme. So, the idea of a pirate retrospective went into hibernation until I discovered it again for this book.

To get myself into this theme, I recalled my childhood. As a child, I loved pirate films and books, like *Treasure Island*. To me, as perhaps to many other boys, pirates were an incredibly exciting topic. I also read a few articles on pirates to get a bigger picture.

When the team is open enough to get into it, a pirate retrospective can be a lot of fun. With a new team, though, you might first try out one of the retrospectives described earlier. But enough words, prepare to board.

5.5.1 Set the Stage

To Set the Stage for a really good pirate retrospective, you should fit the room out with a few things. Give each participant an eye-patch, prop a few sabers up against the wall, have a fishing net with some mussels on the table and you, the facilitator, have a wooden leg. How far you go with this in your retrospective is, of course, entirely up to you. If you're really brave, you could get yourself a parrot for your shoulder from the nearest pet shop. Does this all sound a bit crazy? Yes, I agree, but I'm sure there are teams out there that would engage in it all with pleasure.

After have everyone in the room in the mood, you have the obligatory collecting of piratical terms. As always, I have some examples here:

- Pirate
- Saber
- Pirate ship
- Pirate treasure
- Treasure map

- Treasure Island
- Wooden leg
- Eye patch
- Boarding
- Skull and crossbones flag

I'm sure you'll think up some more. Display these terms, as always, on the wall for the rest of the retrospective.

5.5.2 Gather Data

You are the crew of a pirate ship that has just come to its home port after a successful raiding expedition. You were at sea for a few weeks and wanted to have a little rest before you go out on the next raid. Before you go off to find more victims, you want to review the last expedition. On the whole, your captain was satisfied, but he sees the potential for your improvement as a crew. So that you can better analyze the situation, you divide the raid into four different phases. Initially, at least, you'll examine each of these phases separately. They are:

- Preparation
- Navigation
- The fight
- Quality and division of the booty

You can translate these phases into the real world like this:

- How good was the planning of the last iteration?
- What did the team do to reach its goals?
- How did the implementation go?
- What was the quality of the results of the last iteration and was everyone satisfied with them?

Each of these four phases gets its own piece of flipchart paper. Post them on the walls throughout the room. Now form four groups, and each group stands in front of one of the flipchart papers. The groups now get five minutes in which to write their points on the flipchart paper. When the five minutes are up, the groups rotate clockwise to the next chart. The process is repeated until every group has left their input on every flipchart. In the next step, one member of the group presents all the results from the flipchart in front of him. This is repeated for every chart. This way, you get a good overall picture of the last raid that you can then use to begin looking for the causes of one or two things.

5.5.3 Generate Insights

The first step of the Generate Insights phase is to agree on which points must be most urgently researched. To do that, each group chooses one topic from the flipchart in front of them (that is, with the famous dot voting) and then makes their way clockwise to the next flipchart, and so on. Just one final reminder: The topics chosen don't have to be negative. It can be interesting to find out why something went well so that you have the option of reproducing it. Thus, you get a small surprise effect that can potentially lead to a few new ideas.

You use a special fishbone diagram to analyze possible causes in a pirate retrospective. You can see an example in Figure 5-2. In this diagram, the categories of the main bones are labeled as follows:

- Arming
- Supplies
- Ship
- Enemy
- Crew
- Captain

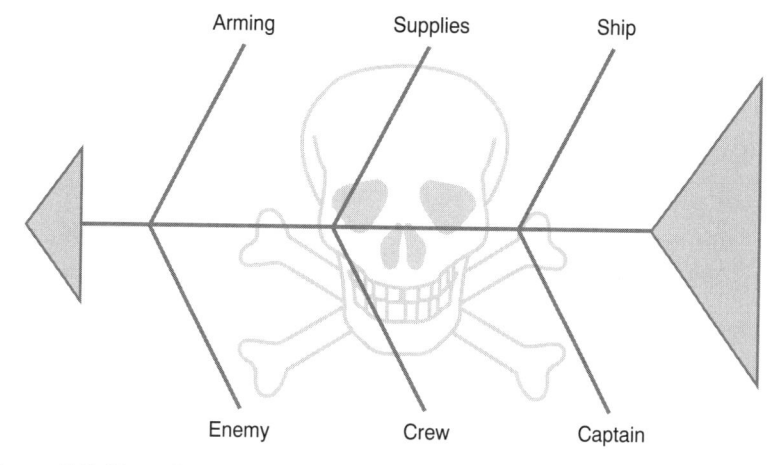

Figure 5-2 Pirate fishbone diagram

This helps you, for one, by keeping you thinking like pirates, and for another, by giving you clear labels for the categories so that you don't have to spend time coming up with them.

At the end of this phase, all the groups present their fishbone diagrams and thus prepare the path for the next phase: the planning of the next raid.

5.5.4 Define Experiments and Hypothesis

Now, you have a better understanding of the last raid and have learned how you might attempt to either avoid the negative or replicate the positive. It's time to make new plans. To do this, divide your next raid into the four categories encountered in the Gather Data phase:

- Preparation
- Navigation
- The fight
- Quality and division of the booty

Again, form four groups (ideally, new groups). Each group takes a phase and collects ideas for the experiments it wants to try. In a second color, they write the respective hypotheses. So, for example, use black for the actual experiment and green for the hypothesis that the experiment will address. After five minutes, the groups rotate clockwise to the next phase, and so on, until they have all contributed to all the phases. Once again, one member of the group presents the collected results.

It is a shame, but you can't carry out all the experiments. Instead, you must all agree on one experiment per phase. To do that, each pirate chooses his favorite experiment per phase by making a mark after it on the flipchart. So, everyone has one vote per phase. The experiments with the most marks become part of the next raid. Now, you are well-prepared for the adventure.

5.5.5 *Closing*

Now and then, it's important to have a retrospective on your retrospectives, and that is why, in closing, having a pirate-style ROTI (Return on Time Invested) can be good. To do this, show the participants a scale with three boats: a death trap with one mast, a normally rigged ship with two masts, and a luxury pirate ship with three masts and everything you could possibly want, cannons and all (see Figure 5-3). Then everyone gets a sticky note in the shape of a ship and can stick it on the scale when he leaves the room. The closer the sticky note to the luxury pirate ship, the better the feedback on the pirate retrospective.

Whether you then invite everyone to a pirate's feast with rum and good music is up to you. You might all simply meet for a cold beer in your favorite bar.

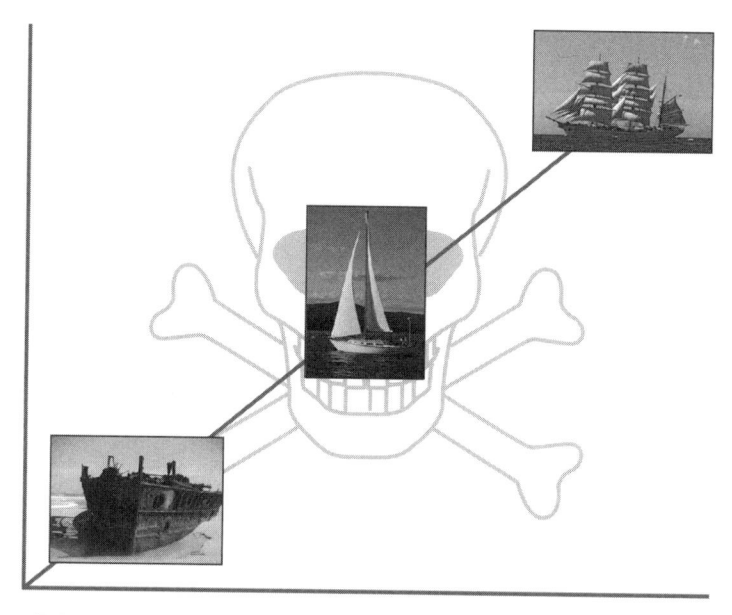

Figure 5-3 Pirate ROTI

Summary

Tired of all the boring retrospective activities you can find online? This is no longer a problem for you. You learned

- How to create your own activities using different metaphors
- How to align the activities so that the whole retrospective makes sense
- How to use the orchestra, soccer, train, kitchen, and pirate metaphors in your retrospectives

As shown in this chapter, creating your own, unique activities is quite easy. You don't want to be creative? No problem. Just use the ideas described here and try them out first. Personally, I'm a big fan of the soccer retrospective, as soccer is quite famous here in Germany. I'm already looking forward to all the email I get from you about your successful pirate or kitchen retrospective. Please let me know about any other cool metaphor you tried with your team. I might try your idea in my next retrospective. Either way, don't forget to have fun.

References

[1] Esther Derby and Diana Larsen. 2006. *Agile Retrospectives: Making Good Teams Great*. O'Reilly UK Ltd.

[2] Ishikawa diagram/Fishbone diagram. https://en.wikipedia.org/wiki/Ishikawa_diagram.

6

Systemic Retrospectives

The first thing I wanted to do when I joined a company a couple of years ago was to observe the teams and get an idea of how they worked. The Scrum framework had been implemented, so I sat in on all the related meetings—the daily stand-up, the sprint review, the sprint planning, and, of course, the retrospectives. After only a short time it became clear to me that it was not going as well as it could and that the Scrum process had started to fall apart in some places. At this point, the company had been working with Scrum for about a year. Team members were trying to work agile in all areas, and they had made great progress. They had begun to introduce TDD (test-driven development), and they had established a continuous integration server as well as all the elements of Scrum. However, it gradually became clear that Scrum doesn't really work unless one key factor is taken into account—the many areas of overlap that concern a team working in a large company. The team will eventually encounter a barrier that seems impossible to overcome. This was palpably clear in the retrospectives.

As I was unsatisfied with the implementation of the retrospectives, I soon offered to lead one. I kept very closely to the five phases, planned creative exercises for each phase, and was for the most part satisfied with how it played out. We had identified problems and looked for their causes and were, in my view, ready to define the measures to be taken. Before we could begin, though, one of the team members pointed out that this was exactly the same result they had gotten in the last retrospective and that he, therefore, couldn't see any point in continuing. The discussion that followed revealed to me for the first time that certain problems originated outside of the team's area of control. Despite that, I insisted that we define some measures to be implemented and that we establish who was responsible for putting them into action and by when. Unfortunately, this had only limited success. I tried, through increasingly creative retrospectives, to achieve better results, but in the end, I had to acknowledge that I was not getting anywhere.

This is a problem that many teams, especially those in large companies, will one day confront if they want to carry out a continuous improvement process. After an energetic first phase, the process grinds to a halt, and it seems as if you simply won't get any further. The reason for this is relatively clear. In the first weeks, the team is concentrating on itself and can quickly, directly, and simply change, create, or get rid of things. Most of these decisions require no external approval and can be enacted quickly. However, after a few months, the whole process grinds to a halt. All the "low-hanging fruits" have been harvested, and addressing issues gets a lot more difficult. The reason lies in the fact that the team is part of a much larger system and is tied up in it through overlaps. Most teams are missing the requisite tools to be able to work successfully in such a system. These tools are called *system thinking* and *complexity thinking*. In the next several sections I articulate what these terms mean and how to apply these techniques in retrospectives.

6.1 Systems

Before I say anything about system thinking, let's first define the word *system*.

The term *system* (from the Greek σύστημα, in ancient Greek pronounced *sýstema*, today *sístima*, composite, made of connected parts; plural *systems*) generally designates a totality of elements that are interrelated or interlinked and that interact in a such way that they can be seen as a coherent unity of task, meaning or use [1].

Examples of systems are, for example, the solar system, clockwork, or engines. The human system is itself comprised of further subsystems like, for example, the circulatory system, the respiratory system, the nervous system, and the digestive system. These subsystems all have a distinct behavior and create, through their cooperation, a new, larger system with a distinct behavior. At the same time, the human being interacts with a social system that can, in turn, be comprised of different subsystems, for example, the family, the club one belongs to, or the company in which one is employed.

A nice metaphor for a system that I will borrow from Rolf Dräther, a fellow Agile coach, is the mobile. The pieces on a mobile all hang more or less together, and you cannot predict in which position the system will come to rest when it is moved. In any case, the stimulus or disturbance—the impulse to movement—must be bearable; that is to say, the system must be able to take it. If the disturbance is too weak, nothing happens. Moved the right amount, the system is put into motion. If the disturbance is too strong, the system either falls from the ceiling or rips and is destroyed.

When we speak of a system, we must also always know where we define the system's borders. This is not at all as easy as it sounds. Jurgen Appelo expressed this well in one of his presentations [2]. Let's say that a group of systemic thinkers go into a bar. The following questions promptly arise:

- What exactly is a bar?
- Are the people sitting here a part of the bar?
- Is the beer a part of the bar?
- What happens when I've drunk my beer? Is it still a part of the bar?
- If I take my beer outside, is it still a part of the bar?
- Is the bar actually a system? If yes, what is the goal of the bar?

You see, it's not so easy. Consider a pile of sand; it isn't a system. This pile of sand has no goal, and you can take sand away or rearrange it, and it doesn't change a thing. The individual parts (the grains of sand) do not interact with one another, and so they do not form a system.

6.1.1 Static and Dynamic

A distinction also exists between static and dynamic systems. Static systems are, in most cases, human-created systems such as organizational systems (the periodic table), classification systems (Linnaean taxonomy), documentation systems (a library), mathematical systems (elementary algebra), and so on. On the other hand, the systems of which the world around us consists—that which we perceive as reality—are all dynamic. They have the program for their own alteration in themselves, so to speak, and are a totality of different unities in interaction.

6.1.2 Complicated and Complex

In addition to being either static or dynamic, systems can also be complicated and complex. Interestingly, we often use these terms interchangeably in our daily lives. Drawing a distinction between these two terms is, however, extremely important because each involves different problem-solving strategies.

Many models describe the difference between complicated and complex, one of which is David Snowden's Cynefin Framework.

The Cynefin model provides a set of contexts that offer a way of determining which explanations and/or solutions might apply. The four contexts are simple, complicated, complex, and chaotic. The chaotic context is, according to Snowden, the condition of "not knowing." Chaos also lies in the area between the other contexts. Snowden suggests specific approaches for working out solutions respective to each context.

I personally prefer a different model to describe this topic: Jurgen Appelo's Structure-Behaviour Model [3, pg. 41]. According to Appelo, considering two distinct features of systems is necessary to articulate the difference between the complicated and the complex. The first feature is the structure of a system and how well one understands it. The two categories are

- Simple = easy to understand
- Complicated = very hard to understand

The second feature is the behavior of a system and how easily one can predict it. The three categories are

- Ordered = completely predictable
- Complex = partly predictable (with the odd surprise)
- Chaotic = virtually unpredictable

Structurally speaking, my socks are "simple" I easily understand how they work. But my son's remote-controlled car is "complicated." To understand how it works, I would first have to take it apart and dedicate still more time to understanding each of the component parts and how they work together. Despite that difference, the behavior of both my socks and the remote-controlled car is easy to predict; they thus have an "ordered" behavior.

My family is also "simple." My wife and I have two sons, and if you wanted to meet us, you could just come over for a coffee or join us for a few days' holiday. The city in which we might spend our joint holiday is not simple, but "complicated." Depending on the size of a city, being able to find one's way confidently around can take years. Despite the difference in structure, the behavior of my family, as well as that of a city, is "complex." I have known my wife for a long time and my children for their whole lives. Yet situations that I am unable to predict are continually cropping up. I can, of course, usually, make reliable estimates of how my family will behave, but only up to a certain point. Without a crystal ball, there will always be surprises.

The lava lamp in our home is also a structurally "simple" system. An electric light warms the wax swimming in the liquid (mostly oil), and the wax then rises in bubbles. As it cools, it sinks again. Despite that simplicity, when a wax bubble rises, I can predict neither what size it will be nor whether it will collide with other wax bubbles. The behavior of the lava lamp is not predictable and is thus "chaotic." The Frankfurt Stock Exchange is also chaotic. Its behavior is not predictable. If it were, the whole stock exchange system would collapse. The Stock Exchange is, as opposed to the lava lamp, extremely complicated structurally. Well, I've never understood how it works, anyway.

According to Appelo's model then, things can be both complex and complicated at the same time; a system can be complicated in its structure and complex in its behavior. It is, however, worth noting that complex systems must not necessarily be complicated. As George E.P. Box states so nicely, "All models are wrong, but some are useful." In the end, these models should help us to classify systems and so understand to what extent they can be influenced and how reliably predictable the outcome of any disturbance is.

6.2 System Thinking

System thinking is a process and not a tool. It is primarily characterized by the attitude that any single event is not the result of a mere single cause, but of the interplay of different elements within a system. Systemically minded people have recognized that any linear cause-and-effect principle can only be partially valid. These people see problems as part of a system and not as its effect.

System thinking offers a collection of tools that help us to understand systems and, from that base, tackle problems within them. Systemically minded people are of the conviction that it only makes sense to solve problems when you know the system and, at best, have visualized it. At the same time, system thinking makes it clear that one is oneself a part of the system and that one's own actions influence other parts of the system in turn. It is interesting just how many people ignore this fact and always see themselves at the end of a chain of causal links. To understand that you are a part of the system is a first step to thinking systemically. In this section, you will be introduced to two tools that will help you to visualize systems and, subsequently, to understand them.

6.2.1 Causal Loop Diagrams

Causal loop diagrams (CLDs) are the most important and fundamental tool for describing systems. The first formal application of these diagrams is credited to Dr. Dennis Meadows. He and his team use CLDs to describe the so-called "World3" Model [4]. A CLD describes how the different variables in a system are causally interrelated and how they mutually affect one another. It consists of several points that represent the different variables. The relationship between these variables is represented by an arrow that indicates either a positive or a negative effect (see Figure 6-1).

Quality ⟶ Customer Satisfaction

Figure 6-1 Causal link

The variables in these diagrams are always nouns and are best when measurable.

6.2.1.1 Same and Opposite Effect

To define the effect one variable has on another, you either write an "s" for same or an "o" for opposite at the head of the arrow. An "s" means that when the variable at the base of the arrow is positively changed, the variable at the other end is also positively changed.

When, for example, as in Figure 6-2, the quality of a product rises, the level of customer satisfaction also rises. What happens to both variables, at either end of the arrow, is thus always the same.

Quality ——————————→ Customer Satisfaction
(s)

Figure 6-2 CLD same effect

An "o" means that when the variable at the base of the arrow is positively changed, the variable at the other end changes in the opposite way; it is negative. So, when the number of leopards in Figure 6-3 rises, there are fewer gazelles at the other end. After all, the leopards' food has to come from somewhere. What happens to one variable is thus always the opposite of what happens to the other.

Leopards ——————————→ Gazelles
(o)

Figure 6-3 CLD opposite effect

When you look at the leopard/gazelle example, you're probably struck by the idea that the number of gazelles must also have an effect on the number of leopards. When there are fewer gazelles, there is less to eat, and so the leopard population will decrease. That hasn't been depicted just yet. You would look in vain for this "loop" in the Figure 6-3, as there are still a few missing elements. These kinds of diagrams have two different basic forms of loops: the balancing loop and the reinforcing loop.

6.2.1.2 Balancing and Reinforcing Loops

In a *balancing* loop, the two variables have a mutual effect on one another. This leads to a kind of stability in that the variables always influence each other in such a way as to hold them in balance. You could, therefore, say that the result is a stable system. In the middle of the balancing loop is a small open circle with an arrowhead that is marked "B" for balancing.

Figure 6-4 shows a simple example of a balancing loop. When the quality of a product rises, the level of customer satisfaction rises, too. This rise in quality will get about, by word of mouth, for example, and in turn, demand will rise. However, the higher demand has, unfortunately, a negative effect on the quality. This is because now a greater number of products must be produced by the same number of workers, lowering the quality. Because of this, the customer satisfaction sinks and demand falls away, leaving workers more time in which to concentrate on quality during the production process. Of course, this example is highly simplified, and certainly a host of other variables exist that influence this system. It does, however, provide a good idea of how a balancing loop works and that's enough for the moment.

Figure 6-4 CLD balancing loop

The opposite of a balancing loop is a *reinforcing* loop. In a reinforcing loop, a system perpetuates itself until it runs into a system boundary that prevents it from continuing. You could call it a vicious cycle, but for the fact that a reinforcing loop isn't necessarily negative. The middle of a reinforcing loop also has a small open circle with an arrowhead, but in this case it is marked with an "R" for reinforcing. To find out whether the CLD system you are building is a balancing loop or a reinforcing one, all you need to do is count the "o" elements. If the "o" count is zero or an even number, then the loop is reinforcing. If the "o" count is an odd number, then it is a balancing one.

Figure 6-5 shows a reinforcing loop in action. It depicts the highly simplified system of a theater. Due to investment, this theater is able to buy better props and hire better actors. Because the performances are now better, the reviews in the press improve (here you could potentially add the variable "quality of the shows").

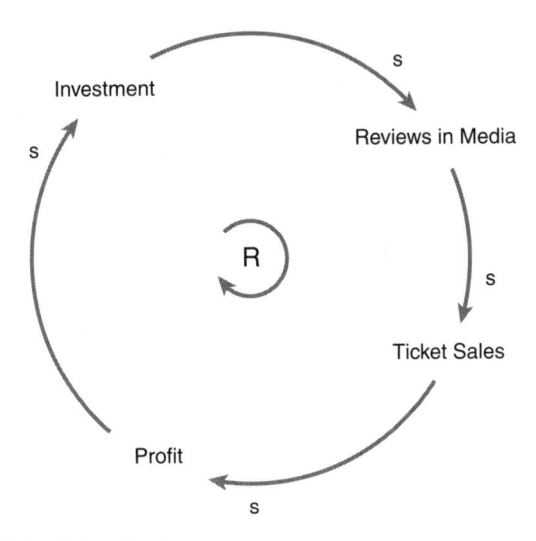

Figure 6-5 CLD reinforcing loop

The improved reviews in the press lead to an increased number of ticket sales, which in turn, yield higher profits that can be reinvested in the theater. It is clear that you cannot limitlessly raise the value of all the variables in the system. At some point, for example, there is no more room in the theater, and you can only sell as many tickets as there are seats. This phenomenon is represented in CLDs with the "constraint" feature.

6.2.1.3 Constraints and Delays

A *constraint* is shown with the letter "c" in the middle of an arrow. Figure 6-6 shows an example of a constraint. As stated earlier, most variables are in some way limited. In this case, you can only sell as many tickets as there are seats available in the theater. When that maximum is reached, the other variables can't go up either. You could, of course, raise the price of the tickets, but before doing that, creating a CLD to determine what the effect of raising those prices would be might be a good idea.

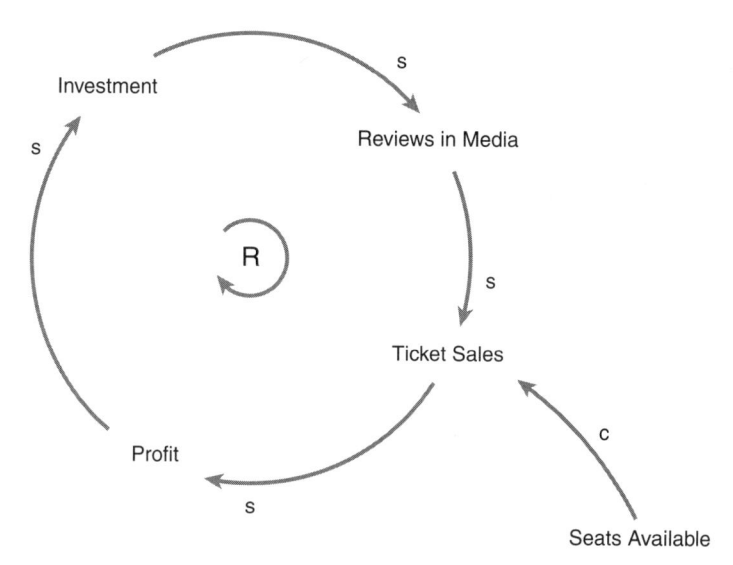

Figure 6-6 CLD constraint

We'll finish our little excursion to CLDs with the *delay*. It should be clear that a change in one variable does not always have an immediate effect on the others. Sometimes it can take a while for the effects to become visible. Figure 6-7 shows a brief example.

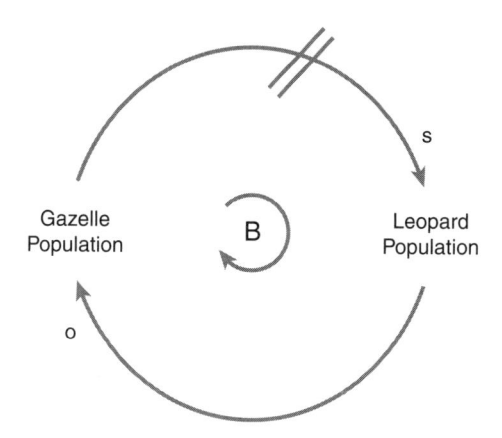

Figure 6-7 CLD delay

The balancing loop in Figure 6-7 shows how the increase of the gazelle population affects the leopard population. When the gazelle population increases and there is thus more for the leopards to eat, there aren't, of course, suddenly more leopards. The gestation period of a leopard cub is about 90 days, and so there is a delay of at least 90 days before the increased gazelle population actually has an effect on the leopard population. On the other hand, the hunting of the gazelles is very swift, and so there is no delay here. The decrease of the gazelle population also has a delayed effect on the leopards because the food shortage does not lead to an immediate reduction of the leopard population.

6.2.1.4 CLD Example

The CLD has more parts, but the ones that shown so far are the most important and most frequently used. Most CLDs can be created with these components. In closing, here is one more example, this time of a larger CLD.

The CLD in Figure 6-8 shows a system in which antelopes and leopards and other predators live and how they affect one another. It all starts at the top left with the rain. This makes the grass grow. The "s" on the arrow tells us that more rain yields more grass. This makes sense. The grass, in turn, has a delayed effect on the antelope population. Here, too, the "s" tells us that both variables rise or fall together. Other predators, like lions or hyenas, for example, also affect the antelope population. These are represented by the variable labeled "other predators" and have an opposite effect on the antelope population ("o"). The more predators, the fewer antelope, and the opposite. If you go to the bottom left, you can see what effect poachers have on the antelope population. As you would expect, the poachers have as much of an opposite effect on the leopards as they have on the antelope. The fewer poachers, the more antelopes/leopards, and the other way around.

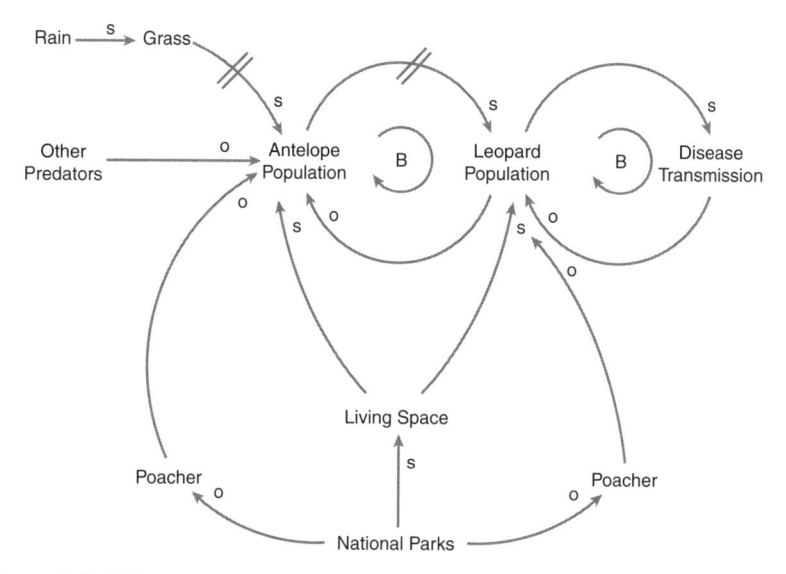

Figure 6-8 CLD example

Finally, comes the variable "living space," which influences the antelope population just as much as the other variables. In this case, the effect is the same ("s"). So, when the living space grows, there is more space for the antelope and their population rises and the other way around. However, living space, which naturally has the same effect on the leopards, is affected by the number of national parks. Here, too, the effect is the same ("s"), so when more national parks exist, more living room for the animals (antelopes and leopards) exists. That national parks and living space also influence the other animals I have left unmarked in this CLD.

Back to the antelope. As described earlier, the antelope population has a delayed, same ("s") effect on the leopard population. The leopard population, though, has an immediate, opposite effect ("o") on the antelope population. The number of the opposite effects ("o") between the antelope and leopards is 1, so we have a balancing loop. The same goes for the loop between the leopard population and the "disease transmission" variable. This is also a balancing loop.

This example represents, again, a highly simplified system, but it does give a good idea of what a CLD looks like. As with every system, you have to draw the line somewhere and decide which variables are important enough to be included in the CLD.

6.2.1.5 CLDs in Retrospectives

After you've been introduced to CLDs, you naturally want to know how you can use them in retrospectives. In this section, we'll look at a few examples from a workshop. The task consisted of finding out how to increase the speed (in Scrum, "velocity") of a team. So, the individual groups worked together on a CLD to show how the individual variables affect one another.

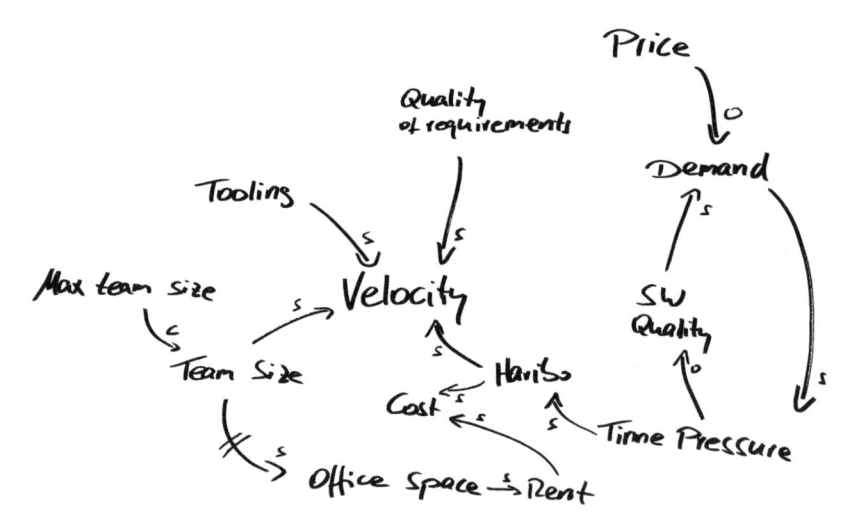

Figure 6-9 Workshop example 1

In the first example in Figure 6-9, four variables have a direct effect on the velocity:

- Quality of the requirements
- The tooling; that is, the materials available
- Team size
- Haribo (gummy bears)

According to this CLD, all four variables have a same effect ("s") on the velocity. So, if the number of gummy bears available to the team increases, the team's velocity increases, too. These variables, which have a direct effect on the velocity, are in turn influenced by additional system variables like the constraints of the maximum team size (left) or costs.

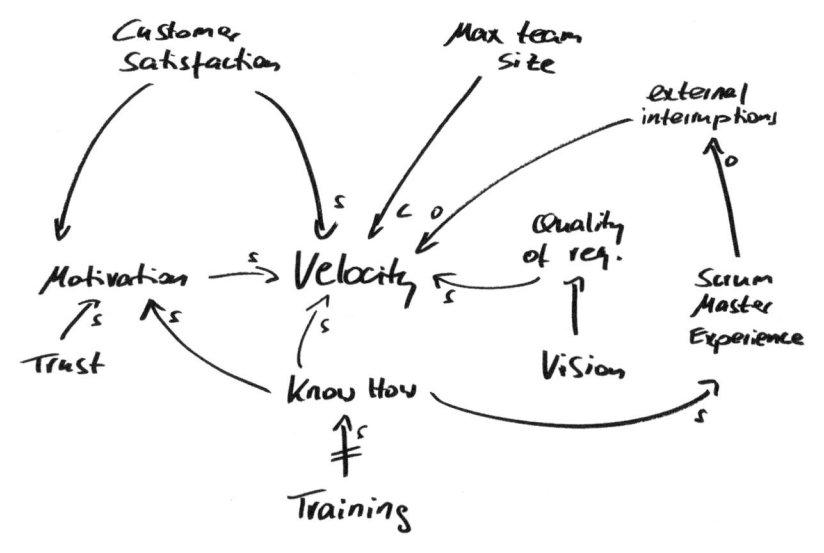

Figure 6-10 Workshop example 2

In the second example in Figure 6-10, six variables affect the velocity:

- Quality of the requirements
- Team size (# Dev = Number of developers)
- Team's know-how
- Team's motivation
- External interruptions
- Customer satisfaction

Two of these variables also appear in CLD 1, so there is a certain consensus. But here, too, the variables that affect velocity are in turn affected by other system variables. For example, the number of developers is dependent on the amount of money available, and the know-how of the team is dependent on potential training. With the help of the CLD, the individual teams have sought to analyze the system in which velocity is embedded and have thus created a better understanding of which factors affect that velocity.

Now that you know the components of CLDs and how they are built, you can use them in retrospectives. They are especially appropriate in two of the phases:

- Generate Insights
- Define Next Experiments

Using the CLD in the Generate Insights phase helps us to better understand why things have happened because it makes the variables of the system visible. In my opinion, though, using it is even more effective in the Define Next Experiments phase, because you can apply it specifically to work out how you can define the most promising possible experiment that will, in the end, fulfill the hypothesis.

> **Practical Tip**
> Keep your worked-out CLDs so you can use them again in the next retrospective. New knowledge and connections that can be used to expand the CLD come up often. See your CLDs as living documentation.

Have another look at the earlier example involving velocity. Let's say that in the retrospective the team has decided to improve its velocity over the coming weeks and months. After creating the appropriate CLD, the team can more easily assess which approach is the most promising. It is also likely that the team is now aware of some variables that they had not considered before the retrospective. Assessing whether any potentially negative effects exist of which the team has been unaware until now is also easier. In short, the team now knows not only the sum of the possibilities but also their effect, if they are enacted.

When I look at the earlier CLDs, there is, in my opinion, one variable in particular that has great potential to increase the velocity in the long term: the quality of the requirements. For one thing, it appears in both CLDs and so seems to be a real problem, and for another, there doesn't seem to be any disadvantage in trying to improve in this area. If you've had anything to do with requirements, then you know for sure that it wouldn't be a simple undertaking, but it is nevertheless worthy of attention.

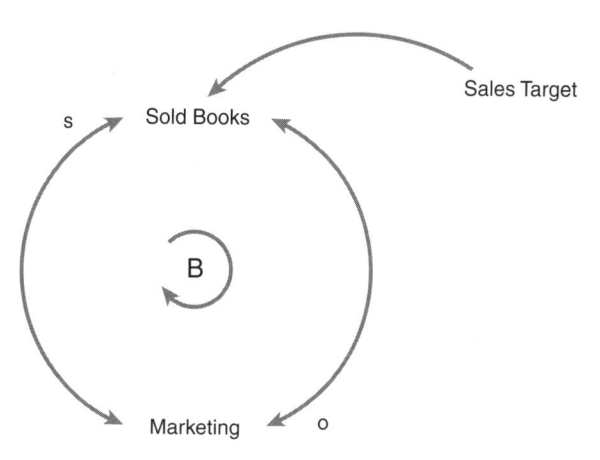

Figure 6-11 CLD example for Practical Tip # 4

Practical Tips

1. Always use nouns for the variable names. Avoid verbs or actions because the arrows already depict what they represent.

2. Use variables that are quantitatively measurable in some way. Using a variable with the name "situation" doesn't make any sense. How can a situation be increased or decreased? "Motivation," on the other hand, would make sense as a variable because motivation can get better or worse. Just how well you can actually measure motivation is a different question.

3. Always take the unintended effects into account as well as those that are intended. For example, when you raise the flow of production, you do indeed get a higher productivity (intended effect), but a simultaneous result could be stress or lower quality (unintended effect). All of these potential effects must be taken into account.

4. Balancing loops always have a goal. This goal must always be a part of the loop. Explicitly including the goal in the CLD makes it clear what you want to achieve (see Figure 6-11).

5. When the connection between two variables requires too much explanation, either rename the variables or insert an intermediate step. Take, for example, the connection between demand and quality in Figure 6-4. Here the question could come up: why does quality suffer because of a rise in demand? Including an intermediate step that was called "pressure on the workers" would be clearer to indicate how the rise in demand influences the quality (see Figure 6-12).

The nearby short tips will help you create better CLDs. But as with everything else, so with CLDs: practice makes perfect. The more CLDs you create, the better you get and the better you can depict different things.

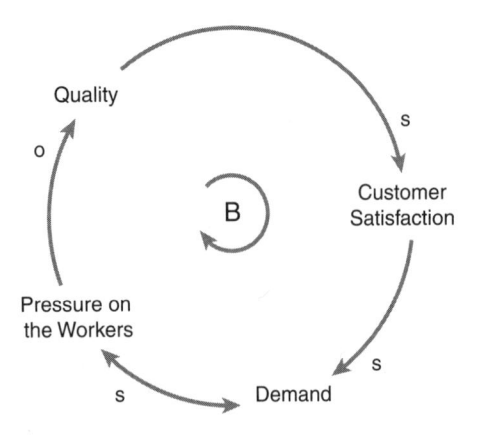

Figure 6-12 CLD Practical Tip #5

6.2.2 Current Reality Tree

The *Current Reality Tree (CRT)* is a tool invented by the now sadly deceased Eliyahu M. Goldratt. It is one of the thought processes that forms part of another of his creations, the Theory of Constraints. If you have never heard of Eliyahu M. Goldratt and want to learn more about this topic, then I heartily recommend his book, *The Goal: The Process of Ongoing Improvement* [5]. It is a very good place to start.

A CRT is not a tree in the true sense of the word, but a digraph. The name was chosen because it sometimes looks like a tree turned upside down. CRTs are related to the 5-Why Method (see Chapter 1, "Retrospectives 101") but are different in that they set up more than one unintended effect as the basis for each graph. Furthermore, they make the connections and interdependencies in a system more visible. You create a CRT in five steps:

1. Collect and consecutively number unintended effects (UEs); that is, all the things in the situation that stand out as being negative.
2. Check that all UEs are clearly comprehensible.
3. Establish causal relations between the different UEs. Which UE is the potential cause or result of another UE?

   This is represented schematically in Figure 6-13. The cause of UE 1 is UE 3. UE 3 is in turn caused by UEs 4 and 5, thus, the ellipse that joins them.

   As yet, UE 2 has been assigned no cause. This happens in step 4.
4. Seek causes for the different UEs (Why?):
   - These may be multiple.
   - Represent "And" connections with an ellipse.
5. Keep looking for further causes, and their causes, until you arrive at the root cause.

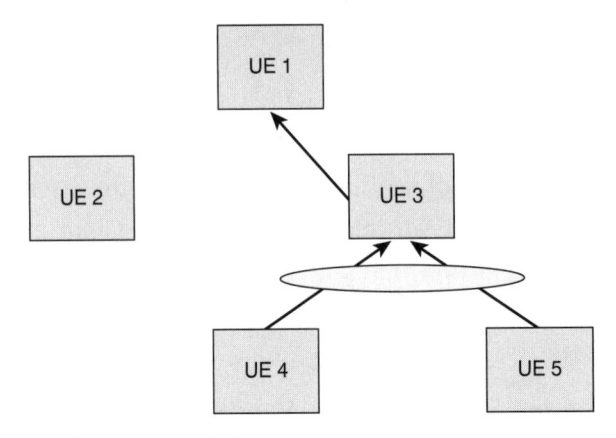

Figure 6-13 CRT after steps 1–3

In Figure 6-14 you see the final CRT, though only schematically, of course. The white boxes represent the established causes. In the end, UE 2 has been placed further down in the CRT. At the bottom is the actual root problem that you would tackle next. Consider this example:

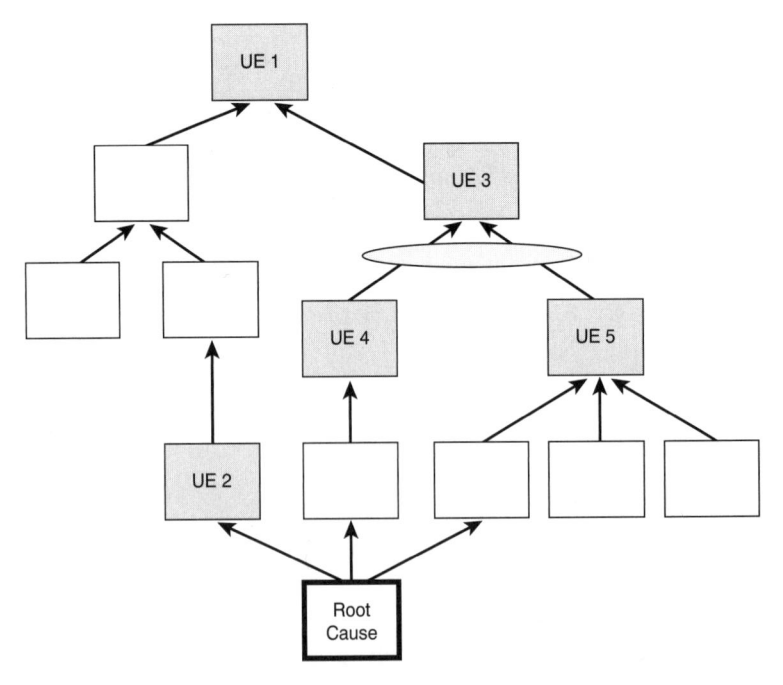

Figure 6-14 CRT after steps 4–5

Let's say that you have the following list of unintended effects (UEs):

- The velocity is too low.
- The quality of the software is poor.
- The customer is unhappy.
- Developers are resigning in spades.

If you were to take these UEs and carry out steps 1–3 as described earlier, the CRT would look like Figure 6-15. The causes of the customer's unhappiness are, among others, UE 1 and UE 2—in other words, the slow velocity and the poor quality of the software.

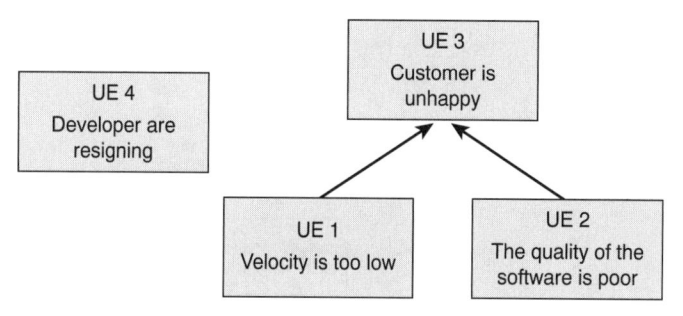

Figure 6-15 CRT example after steps 1–3

UE 4 (Developers resigning) couldn't be tied into the diagram until now because the other UEs couldn't be seen as direct causes. To find these causes, you carry out steps 4–5 as described earlier.

You can see the result in Figure 6-16. In total, nine further causes have been added to the four UEs. UE 4 (our developers) has made it to the top of the diagram. According to the CRT, the causes of many developers leaving the company are the higher pressure on the developers and a lack of opportunities for professional development (bottom right), which is also one of the main problems. The cause of the higher pressure is mainly the customer's dissatisfaction. For this pressure there are, according to the CRT, three reasons: the already identified UEs 1 and 2 and the lack of inclusion of the client. The client feels neglected by our company, principally because contact with the client has been practically non-existent. This lack of contact with the client has been identified as a further main reason for the whole dilemma.

Now let's have a look at UE 1, the low velocity. The cause of this is, above all, the poor quality of the standards, which is, in turn, a result of the failure to include the client. The cause of the consistent problems with building software and the fact that the company is seldom in a position to build a stable version has also been identified. This is caused as much by the lack of automatized testing as by the lack of an integration environment in which to carry out these tests and build the software at regular intervals. This lack of an integration environment has been identified as a further main reason for the problems.

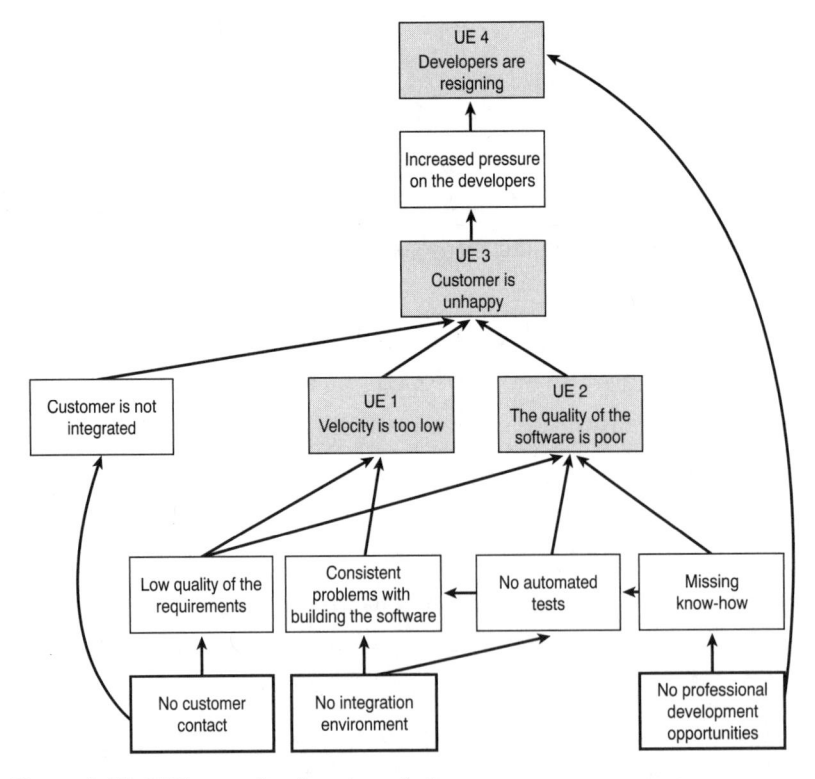

Figure 6-16 CRT example after steps 4–5

Finally, let's look at UE 2, the poor quality of the software. This has three main causes: the poor quality of the standards, the lack of automated testing, and the lack of know-how among the employees. In the end, each of these causes can be traced back to the three main causes that have been identified:

- No contact with the clients
- No integration environment
- No professional development opportunities

These main causes are, in the end, the starting points for further action in the company. As you can see, a CRT is a very powerful tool for analyzing a situation and for finding starting points for solutions. That is why it is outstandingly useful for retrospectives.

> **Practical Tip**
>
> Special software for building CRTs is available, but you can also use more general software such as Microsoft Visio. In any case, I recommend creating CRTs in teams, and this is much more effective when done with the help of sticky notes and a whiteboard. The UEs and other causes go on the notes, which you can then connect with lines on the whiteboard. The advantage of this combination is that you can easily move sticky notes (and that will happen more than once) and quickly redraw a line on the whiteboard. In this way, you can collaboratively work on a CRT and discuss the connections.

You can use CRTs to great effect in the Generate Insights phase of retrospectives. They are, in my opinion, an ideal substitute for the 5-Why question method and are especially effective if you're not making progress with other methods. A CRT delivers just the right starting points to use in further phases of a retrospective.

Also, the team will become aware of the system in which it works and will offer up many new options and ideas for how to proceed in a given situation.

6.2.3 Limitations of System Thinking

As a discipline in its own right, system thinking is relatively young. It was developed in the 1980s and made popular principally by the book *The Fifth Discipline* by Peter Senge [6]. As described earlier in this chapter, it is a particular way of thinking to solve problems. System thinking has made its primary contribution in the analysis of problematic systems and has been less focused on problematic people, which is the greatest weakness of this way of thinking.

Social complexity is the investigation of complexity in social systems. However, traditional system thinking has often ignored the fact that you cannot realistically analyze and adjust social behavior [7]. Critics of system thinking argue that the simulation of organizations with simplified models, or the depiction of teams and people with circles and arrows, can lead management to mistakenly believe that they can use this method to analyze, modify, and finally, steer their organization in the "right" direction. System thinking is not concerned with linear relationships but does hold firmly to the idea that upper management can in some way create the "right" kind of organization, which will deliver the "right" kind of results [3, pg. 49]. The twenty-first century is the century of complexity. It is the century in which managers realize that they must understand how things grow, and not how they are built, to be able to affect social complexity [3, pg. 49].

In our working world, we most often have to deal with complex, adaptive systems—that is, with teams composed of interacting parts (mostly people)—which have the opportunity to adapt to their environment and learn from their experiences. Even in a small team, one in which the individual team members know each other well, you can never say with 100% certainty how the system will react to internal and external stimulation. I have known my wife for a long time now, and yet she still surprises me today. As soon as you have to consider human beings and their social interaction in a system, it becomes difficult to grasp with purely systemic thinking. To create a CLD or CRT in which this social complexity is depicted is almost impossible.

Despite all of these arguments, my opinion is that system thinking and its accompanying tools are very useful. They often open up completely new views on a system from which new possibilities can arise. They give an initial idea of which variables in a system are available and help to define new experiments. "Experiment" is the key word. You must always be clear about the fact that you can only depict an approximation of reality with a CLD or CRT. Therefore, all the measures that are taken on the basis of these tools can only be experiments. This is one of the reasons why I call the fourth phase "Define Next Experiments." That is also the reason why I find the use of hypotheses to be so important. You can never predict with 100% certainty what the effect of the interaction with the system, your company, will be, even when the CLD is appropriately complex. In the end, everything is an experiment to test the hypothesis that you have worked out. It is crucial that you check your hypothesis at regular intervals, as doing so will keep you on the right track. Keeping that in the back of your mind ensures that system thinking is a thoroughly valuable tool.

It goes without saying that there is also a particular approach that takes into consideration the weakness in system thinking described in this section. This approach is called complexity thinking.

6.3 Complexity Thinking

As with system thinking, there is no unified definition of *complexity thinking*. I understand complexity thinking as a further form of system thinking, which also considers social complexity. Complexity thinking holds that systems in which social relationships play a role are not controllable. It recognizes that you cannot simply build a team that will exactly do what you've thought up and described in the models and plans. On the contrary, all you can do is affect such a system with experiments and then watch how it behaves. I like to describe this as dancing with the system. You take a step, let the system respond and then take the next step. Sometimes small, local changes have a giant effect on the whole organization (the so-called butterfly effect), and sometimes apparently huge changes have no effect whatsoever. Causes and effects are therefore not always discernible. Solutions that have worked outstandingly in one company can lead to catastrophic situations in another. Solutions can never be carried over one to one between organizations or even teams.

In short, complex systems are rarely predictable. Planning tools that have worked well in the past can often be applied in only a limited way in today's world. It is thus even more important to structure your organization so that you are better prepared for these complex environments and can react to them with greater flexibility.

6.3.1 Martie—The Management 3.0 Model

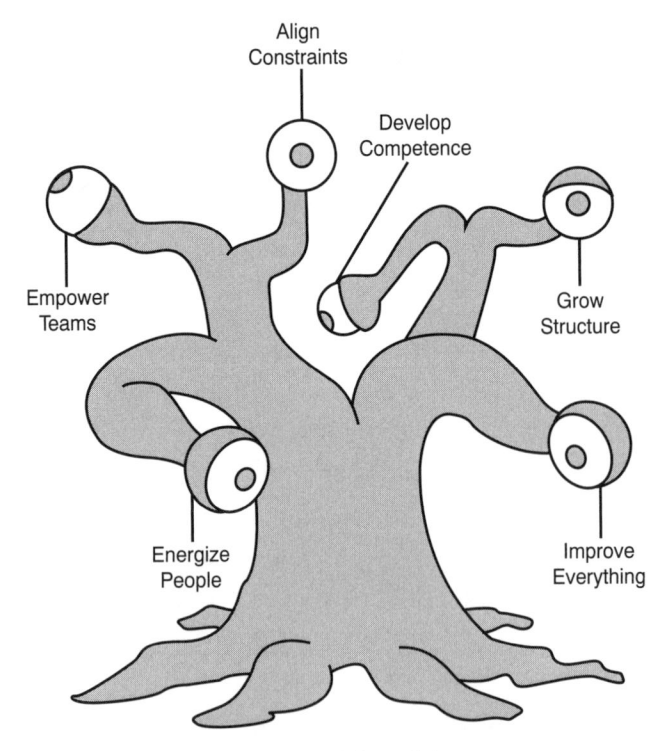

Figure 6-17 Martie—the Management 3.0 model

In his book *Management 3.0* [3], Jurgen Appelo articulates a model that can help with complex systems (see Figure 6-17). The model describes six different views on organizations and suggests different techniques for structuring a growing, self-organizing and adaptable organization.

- **Energize People**

  The people in a network are the only ones in a position to automatically adapt to the situation. That is why it is important to create a motivating environment in which people in a system can give their best.

- **Empower Teams**

  Self-management can only work if teams have the power and authority to make decisions. That is why it is important for management to delegate that power to the people below them, the people who, in most cases, know better how to solve a problem. After all, they do spend all day doing it.

- **Align Constraints**

  Of course, you don't want a system in which everyone does what he wants, and that can move in any direction. That is why it is important to set clear boundaries and to design a vision with which all can identify and that sets the team's energy free.

- **Develop Competence**

  Good organizations are made of good teams and so, in the end, of the best-educated people. That is why it is important to make sure that the individuals in an organization continue to develop and build competencies.

- **Grow Structure**

  For an organization to grow, the right structures must be to hand. That is why it is important to structure the organization to be as flexible as possible. This is the only way to ensure that an organization can grow without becoming a victim of its own structure.

- **Improve Everything**

    This is related to the term *kaizen culture*, a culture that places emphasis on continued improvement. Only when one continues to improve can one exist in the future.

Like the ABIDE model (discussed later in this chapter), the Management 3.0 model shows different areas that can be affected with targeted experiments. You can use this model to carry out retrospectives at a team level, but its potential is most fully realized at the management level. A retrospective based on the Management 3.0 model could look as described in the following sections.

6.3.1.1 Set the Stage

In the Set the Stage phase, you introduce Martie, briefly explain the six views, and then choose one them; for example, Energize People.

6.3.1.2 Gather Data

In the Gather Data stage use a round of brainstorming to identify all the things that:

- hinder the team members from doing their work
- have a demotivating effect on the team or individuals
- limit creativity
- reduce the transparency of an organization
- reduce the diversity of a team

In short, identify all of those things that hinder the creation of a healthy, motivating, and inspiring atmosphere in which people enjoy committing themselves fully.

6.3.1.3 Generate Insights

The Generate Insights step is about finding out why these things exist and how they are caused. Only when I understand why something is the way it is can I effectively look for alternatives. Sometimes, it simply is that things have always been that way and have never been questioned. If you know the original causes for the impediments listed in the preceding step, then you will later have the opportunity of demonstrating that they are potentially no longer necessary. Thus, you create the basis for the next phase.

6.3.1.4 Define Experiments and Hypothesis

How can you get rid of the impediments collected at the beginning? For example, what must you do to create more transparency? What experiments can you carry out that will give the system more energy? On the basis of the collected insights, you can decide on targeted experiments and their hypotheses. What effect these will have and whether or not they turn out to be positive you will learn, at the latest, in the next retrospective.

6.3.1.5 Closing

At the end of such a retrospective, ask yourself whether the Management 3.0 model has given you the advantage that you hoped for. If you're satisfied with the results, then you can also decide at this point which of the six views you want to use in the next retrospective.

6.3.2 The ABIDE Model

In complex systems, the possibility of checking and adjusting the system always exists. But which screws and wheels can you turn to affect the system? What lever is there that you can pull? What parameters haven't occurred to you yet? The ABIDE model was created to identify these parameters.

The ABIDE model was developed by David Snowden and is an acronym for the things that can be affected in a complex system. David Snowden is an expert in the field of complexity thinking and its practical application in organizations. He developed the Cynefin-model [8] described earlier in this chapter. ABIDE stands for

- **Attractors:** Things, ideas, or people to which the system responds positively
- **Barriers:** Define the system's boundaries
- **Identity:** The roles and responsibilities in the system
- **Diversity:** The differences between the team members in the system
- **Environment:** The system environment

6.3.2.1 Attractors

Attractors are things, ideas, or people that are attractive to others and to which they are drawn. By changing what the people in a system find attractive, you can affect the dynamic of the system itself. Here are some examples of attractors:

- A well-known person from outside the organization who talks about a new idea. Because the person is well-known, the new idea is automatically more attractive.
- A prize for achieving a goal.
- A new, attractive position in the company.
- A well-crafted product vision.
- Recognition from other team members.

There are no limits to the imagination here. You don't have to stick to existing attractors, but can also define new attractors or make current ones even more attractive.

6.3.2.2 Barriers

Barriers define the edges of the system and therefore also define what a part of the system is and what it is not. If you move the barriers, you change the parts of the system and, in turn, the dynamics of the system. Here are some examples of barriers:

- The time allocated for a task.
- The physical barrier of a wall between team rooms.
- The definition of the project team. Who is and is not a part of the team?
- The person in the middle who is hindering me from making direct contact with another person.

So, physical barriers exist as well as barriers that originate in company or project structures. Barriers can in most cases be moved and extended and sometimes also added. In the end, each barrier affects the system and the agents who interact with it.

6.3.2.3 Identity

Identity means the roles and responsibilities within a system. If you change someone's role, and thus their identity, you simultaneously change the identity of the team of which that person is a part. A person can have several identities, and context only determines which identity dominates. Here are some examples of identity:

- The identity of a group. Give them more responsibility, and you change their identity.
- The identity of a person, which can likewise be changed by the addition or subtraction of responsibilities.
- Identities are always tied to people in some way. A variety of ways exist to affect the identity of a person and thus change the behavior of the system.

6.3.2.4 Diversity

Diversity is a broad term. Primarily, it means different cultures, opinions, and ways of behaving, as well as different genders. A certain amount of diversity is necessary for a team to be able to organize itself. Homogeneous groups are rarely innovative because innovation requires constructive dialogue between people who think differently. On the other hand, too much diversity can make the potential for conflict too big and can make it difficult for the team even to listen to each other, never mind work productively together. Here are some examples of diversity:

- Different cultures
- People with different experience, that is, in small or large firms
- Different kinds of technical expertise

Changing the diversity of a system also leads to a different dynamic. The diversity can be increased or decreased to reach the desired effect.

6.3.2.5 Environment

The environment of a system can be physical or cultural in nature, from the furnishing of a workplace with modern hardware to a company's culture. Here are some examples:

- The work environment, that is plants, the spatial setup of the offices (small or large room offices), or simply the technical setup.
- The culture of an organization. Is it more conservative or liberal? How transparent is the company decision-making process? Are there flexible work times or the possibility of working from your home office?

- Each change in the environment influences the system and causes it to react differently. The possibilities for change in the environment are also manifold.

The ABIDE model is outstandingly suited for use in a retrospective. Just when you can't make any progress and seem to have run out of ideas, the ABIDE model can help you discover new possibilities and start new experiments.

> **Practical Tip**
>
> Starting to use the ABIDE model to find the possible causes of problems in the Generate Insights phase is best. You can then use it in the Define New Experiments phase to look for new starting points for affecting the system.

The ABIDE model is best used in the following way:

1. Introduce the ABIDE model and its five elements. Give a few examples for each element (Set the Stage).
2. Create groups of 3–5 people (max 5 persons per group).
3. Prepare a sheet of flipchart paper for each element and hang them around the room. If you have enough flipcharts, just leave the sheets on the pad.
4. Have each group stand next to one of the element papers; for example, Barriers.
5. Each group gets two minutes to fill its flipchart with ideas about its respective element (Gather Data).
6. After the two minutes, the teams move on to the next element and repeat step 5.
7. After five rounds, the brainstorming ends.
8. Use the collected data and analyze it e.g. with a Fishbone diagram (Generate Insights).

9. Define a potential experiment and hypothesis for all five of the elements.

10. Select the two most promising experiments to be addressed in the next iteration of your team (Define experiments and Hypothesis).

Keep these lists after the retrospective so that you can turn to them again in the next one.

Summary

In this chapter, you learned how to apply system and complexity thinking to your retrospectives. The following topics were covered:

- Defining what a system is and is not
- The difference between complicated and complex systems
- The use of causal loop diagrams and how to apply them to retrospectives to identify new levers to pull
- The Current Reality Tree and why it can be helpful in your context
- How to use Marty the Management 3.0 model to your retrospectives
- Using the ABIDE model and why it is useful

With these tools, you are now armed to tackle the more difficult areas of change in your organization. Having a basic understanding of systems and complexity thinking is beneficial to be able to define meaningful experiments. However, never forget: You are working in a complex adaptive system; you'll never know whether you'll succeed beforehand. No worries if an experiment doesn't work; that's why it is called an experiment. Just try your next idea until the issue is solved or not that relevant anymore.

References

[1] Wikipedia. 2017. *System*. https://en.wikipedia.org/wiki/System

[2] Jurgen Appelo. 2011. *Complexity Thinking or Systems Thinking*. http://de.slideshare.net/jurgenappelo/complexity-thinking

[3] Jurgen Appelo. 2011. *Management 3.0—Leading Agile Developers, Developing Agile Leaders*. Addison-Wesley Longman.

[4] Wikipedia. 2017. *Causal Loop Diagram*. https://en.wikipedia.org/wiki/System

[5] Eliyahu M. Goldratt. 2012. *The Goal: A Process of Ongoing Improvement*. North River Pr Inc.

[6] Peter Senge. 2006. *The Fifth Discipline—The Art and Practice of a Learning Organization*. Crown Business.

[7] David Snowden. 2005. *Multi-ontology Sense Making: A New Simplicity in Decision Making*. Management Today, Yearbook, Vol. 20.

[8] Wikipedia. 2017. *Cynefin Framework*. https://en.wikipedia.org/wiki/Cynefin_framework.

7

Solution-Focused Retrospectives

By Veronika Kotrba MC and Dr. Ralph Miarka MSc

The goal of most retrospectives is to work together as a group to find changes that will lead to a better future. In our experience of retrospectives, however, a lot of time is often spent on discussing the "bad" past. The result of this is that the participants spend an insufficient amount of time discussing their desired future. This gives the impression that no significant steps forward have been taken and, as a consequence, the participants of these retrospectives always report feeling frustrated and demotivated.

In contrast to this, Steve de Shazer and Insoo Kim Berg's solution-focused approach concentrates on the "better" future. In our view, it offers an alternative and effective way to lead retrospectives.

In this section, we will introduce the attitudes, principles, and tools of solution-focused therapy and show how we have implemented them in retrospectives. We use, like Derby and Larsen [1], five steps and call them:

- Opening
- Set Goals
- Find Meaning
- Initiate Action
- Check Results

Rather than focus on analyzing problems, this approach directs our attention toward a better future, full of potential solutions.

In addition to solution-focused brief therapy, Frankl's teachings on meaning [9], as well as the positive psychology of Fredickson [4] and Losada and Heaphy [5], also play a role in solution-focused retrospectives as we describe them.

7.1 The Solution-Focused Approach

The solution-focused approach [2] originates in family therapy and was developed in the 1970s by a research team centered on Steve de Shazer and Insoo Kim Berg. The couple worked with their clients at their Institute in Milwaukee, Wisconsin, the Brief Family Therapy Center (BFTC). There, they observed that some clients were able to develop realistically implementable ideas to improve their situations more quickly than others. The duration of these patients' treatment was, therefore, significantly shorter than that of those who found it more difficult to find first steps toward solutions. The researchers became interested in what these people were doing differently. What they discovered later formed the basis of solution-focused brief therapy.

What follows is an introduction to what seem to us to be some of the most important principles of solution-focused work.

7.1.1 Problem Talk Creates Problems, Solution Talk Creates Solutions

The most important tool in solution-focused work is language [3]. Language creates reality and change. That is, the more precisely you describe a situation, the more you create the experience of actually being in that situation.

When you describe an unpleasant event from your past in as much detail as you can recall, you begin to physically feel the same way that you did at the time. Your body's reactions are thus similar in the present to what they were in that past moment. You have the impression of re-living the same experience.

Conveniently, this also works for situations you have not experienced yet. However, you should then focus on the positives. The more precisely you describe your picture of the desired future, the more you will physically feel now, as you will in that future. That present feeling has the effect of pulling you, like a magnet, in the direction of your goal. Only if you can formulate what the goal (the desired future) looks like, will you be able to find a path toward that goal and, in the end, meet it.

> **Practical Tip**
>
> The precise description of the desired goals can be supported, for example, with the following questions:
>
> - What is your goal? What do you want to achieve?
> - How will you know that you have achieved your goal? What will be different? What else?
> - What will you do differently when you have reached your goal?
> - How will other people recognize that you have reached your goal?
> - How will they react to the changes?
> - What do those reactions mean to you?

There is another, in our view, important and fundamental principle of the solution-focused approach based on the recognition that language creates reality: We put our focus on the better future!

7.1.2 Focus on the Better Future

Steve de Shazer's starting point was the idea that a problem and its solution do not always stand in direct relation to one another.

What he meant was that an exact knowledge of the source of a problem or an unsatisfactory situation does not itself contribute to the definition of steps toward improvement.

Who is to blame? How did it get this far? What mistakes were made? Questions like these do not lead to an improvement of the overall situation.

A focus on the negative past has little to be recommended: For one thing, it leads us into to a kind of problem-trance, because we re-experience in the present the feelings of the past (powerless, unhappy, angry, and so on), and for another, it doesn't even help us in our search to find steps in the direction of improvement.

The past is irrelevant; the desired goal for the present and the future is the only thing that is important in finding a solution. We believe that people can change and can freely choose to do what they did one way yesterday differently today.

Having a look at the past still makes sense, even from the solution-focused point of view. However, when we do so, we are not looking for the causes of problems, but for those moments in which things were better.

7.1.3 No Problem Happens All the Time; There Are Always Exceptions That Can Be Utilized

The researchers in Milwaukee were especially surprised by the observation about problem exceptions. In every situation, no matter how bad, there are moments in which the problem is less, or even not at all, perceptible. These moments, and, above all, what they represent, are important guides to a rapid improvement of the overall situation. That is why it pays to look out for them and give them special attention.

We can find out what was different in those better moments and use this knowledge in the future.

7.1.4 If It Works, Do More of It

What has worked well once, might well work again. This statement implies three ideas that we believe are particularly motivating:

- We have apparently, even in the past, done things well. So, it seems that we are in a position to actively bring about improvements ourselves.
- We do not need to be overly creative to find first ideas for reaching our goal—we already know something that works well.
- Doing *everything* differently to reach our better future is by no means necessary. So, a lot of what we already do should, or might, stay the same.

> **Practical Tip**
>
> The following questions can help you in the search for positive exceptions from the past:
>
> - When was the situation a little better for you?
> - Are there examples in the past that were similar to your desired future? If yes, what are they?
> - What was different in those moments?
> - What did you contribute that made those moments possible?
> - Who else contributed, and how?

You might be thinking, "And what happens if what worked before doesn't work anymore?" Might this way of thinking not also lead to a depressing dead end? Well, yes, of course; circumstances can exist that prevent the repetition of strategies from being successful. De Shazer's answer to that is, in keeping with his minimalist nature.

7.1.5 If It's Not Working, Do Something Different

"Okay, but what?" was what I thought when I first heard that statement. Today, I know how unbelievably important it is for me and for my progress!

Perhaps you have had something of the same experience: When I work out that, logically, a certain approach to solving a problem must work, I am well and truly ready to bang my head against the metaphorical wall and, if my plan doesn't work, will convince myself that any randomly encountered circumstances were responsible. In the absolute certainty that the next attempt will work, I keep using the same strategy again and again on the same wall. And only when, figuratively speaking, my nose is bloody, do I begin to admit that there might be a completely different way to the desired goal.

To find a new approach, it is, of course, necessary to know the goal you are working toward. It is also helpful to be brave and open to creative and completely new ways of thinking. At first, they don't even need to sound realistic—they might even be crazy, irrational, and fantastic. The wildest of ideas often hide creative and practically applicable possibilities.

> **Practical Tip**
>
> The following questions can be helpful in supporting the development of these new ideas:
>
> - Who in your surroundings knows you/your situation particularly well?
> - What would he/she say was the best way for you to reach your goal?
> - If you had every conceivable possibility without limits, how would you reach your goal?

This isn't about creating in your head the coolest, most involved fantasy story. Absolutely the opposite: Creativity is most in demand when you're trying to keep it simple.

7.1.6 Small Steps Can Lead to Big Changes

Very often, the smallest things can lead to big changes. For example, an altered seating position, a different light or a similar modification in a room can be responsible for a changed atmosphere in a meeting. A simple and sincere "thank you" can change a relationship. A genuine smile can improve a whole day. Surely, you, too, have experienced the way a small intervention has had a large effect. What examples can you think of?

In solution-focused work, we use the instrument of *scaling* to help us define small steps. We can use a 10-part scale to visualize the starting point (that is, the present), the point at which the goal is reached, and the steps to be taken in that direction. This form of visualization helps us order our thoughts, bring them into sequence, and thus create a plan for their implementation.

How exactly scaling questions work and how you can implement them in your solution-focused meetings will be described a little later.

Solution-focused work is supported very intensively with questions. Like an old piece of wisdom reminds us: The one who asks, leads. Solution-focused questions are the most important tool in our box. The thoughts and personal attitudes that follow will help you to actually implement them effectively.

7.1.7 Focus on Strength and Skills

Instead of concentrating on the mistakes and weaknesses of the person to whom we are speaking, we focus on their strengths and skills. We decide for ourselves, whenever we see or hear something, where we want to place our attention—on that which is good or that which is bad.

The decision we make is based on our expectations, which are influenced by our experience. So, when Mr. B shows up late to the meeting for what feels the hundredth time, we find it difficult to assume that he did his best to be punctual this time.

However, we can choose instead to be happy about the fact that all are now present. We can also notice that this time Mr. B only made us wait for five minutes instead of the usual ten. If he should once appear punctually, it makes sense, in private and after the meeting, to ask what difference it made to him to be there from the beginning this time.

Our focus on apparent abilities and skills shows the person to whom we are talking which tools they already possess that can enable them to effect change actively.

7.1.8 Understand and Trust That Each Person Is an Expert in His or Her Own Situation

No one knows what you need better than you do yourself! And no one knows what your colleague needs better than your colleague! On one hand, recognizing this should remind us not to read things into the statements or actions of others. On the other, it is a relief to all of those who believe that they must solve the problems of others, because it means that only those who have a problem can find the right solution!

So, the facilitator's task is not to solve all the problems that arise. Rather, he should help others find their own ways of solving them. Solutions generated by people themselves are implemented significantly more often than those that are the result of external advice.

You, too, are probably familiar with situations in which well-intended advice simply could not help you make progress—perhaps because the person who wanted to help you simply didn't know important details about your situation or hadn't interpreted them helpfully. This leads us to what is possibly the most challenging basic attitude of solution-focused work: the attitude of not knowing.

7.1.9 Keep the Attitude of Not Knowing

We have all had many experiences in our lives up to this point. Understandably then, we feel like experts in the most varied of fields. Whenever we see or hear something, we build hypotheses on the basis of our experience. However, these hypotheses often prevent us from asking about the implied context and the intended goal of an approach we observe because we believe we already know the answer!

In the solution-focused approach, we are aware of that fact. However, you cannot prevent yourself from making hypotheses. The more you try, the less you are able to listen to other people. We then miss important information about potential steps toward a solution because our focus is on ourselves and our hypotheses rather than the person to whom we are listening. A significantly more helpful approach is to accept your own thoughts and hypotheses, to put them aside, and to remain open to and curious about answers that you might not expect.

This approach helps us to ask the right questions in a helpful way. Our questions help people to find their own approach, instead of manipulating them to think in a direction that corresponds with our experience. Assuming the attitude of not knowing requires trust in others' expertise in their own situation and restraint in giving advice and patience. That is why it is, for many people, the most difficult of the basic attitudes to acquire.

7.1.10 Be Patient and Confident

Getting people to find their own, effective, and sustainable solutions any faster is simply impossible! Questions stimulate a thought process, and getting an answer can take a really long time. Maintaining this silence is sometimes difficult and uncomfortable. To interrupt it with another question, for example, means to break off the thought process that you had previously so masterfully triggered.

An important rule for a situation like this is: When you have asked a question, wait until you get an answer, however long it takes! Just try it! You'll see that you'll get, sooner or later, a considered, sometimes surprising answer. If when you get an answer, you hear that your question wasn't understood or couldn't be answered, then it's time to re-formulate the question or to head in a different direction with your questions. Just between us, having managed to hold the silence often feels really good. Enjoy it!

It might now be interesting to compare the Prime Directive for retrospectives with the principles and attitudes of the solution-focused approach that we've just described.

7.1.11 The Prime Directive of Retrospectives

Regardless of what we discover, we understand and truly believe that everyone did the best job they could, given what they knew at the time, their skills and abilities, the resources available, and the situation at hand.

At the end of a project, everyone knows so much more. Naturally, we will discover decisions and actions we wish we could do over. This is wisdom to be celebrated, not judgment used to embarrass.

When you read this statement of Norman Kerth with a solution-focused lens, understand it less as a guide to action than as a fundamental attitude. After all, simply reading it out cannot make it real. Instead, we recommend devoting a whole workshop to making the content of the Prime Directive an experience and thus bringing that experience into the team's everyday work. To embrace the attitudes and principles of the solution-focused approach is to understand the Prime Directive as a logical conclusion of that approach.

In the next part of this chapter, we introduce you to one of many ways that you can use the principles of the solution-focused approach in a retrospective.

7.2 A Solution-Focused Retrospective in Five Steps

One of the most influential texts on the topic of team retrospectives is the book *Agile Retrospectives* by Derby and Larsen. In this book, they introduce a five-stage structure for leading retrospectives. Having also found a five-stage structure to be useful, we have borrowed from their model in creating ours. In the following pages we will lead you through these five phases of a solution-focused retrospective:

- Opening
- Set Goals
- Find Meaning
- Initiate Action
- Check Results

7.2.1 Opening

The goal of our opening is to make creative and team-oriented work possible. Additionally, we would like the team members to immediately start concentrating on functioning aspects that might be helpful for future work.

In *Positivity* [4] Fredrickson describes "The Secret of Successful Teams." She presents research [5] by indicating that successful teams are composed of people who make six times more positive statements than negative ones. Furthermore, these teams have higher group connectivity. That is, the team members concentrate more on the group than they do to themselves. Moreover, when the team communicates, there are just as many questions asked as positions defended, and the attention of these teams is directed as much outside as inside. These teams also demonstrate that they are more flexible and resilient than comparable groups. Fredrickson describes how positive thinking expands horizons, opens us up to novelty, creates new resources, and develops resilience. Here is a list of potential interventions:

- **Intervention: Something True and Positive**

    These insights motivate us to create a similar work environment. For that reason, we start a solution-focused retrospective with having each team member say something true and positive about his or her own work. This simple intervention leads to more creativity, engagement, and positive thinking during the whole meeting.

- **Intervention: Chain Question**

    To develop the group's connectivity, we use a technique that we call chain questions. You ask the person next to you (person 1) to tell you something true and positive about his or her own work. After they have answered you, they then make the same request of the person next to them (person 2), and so on.

    This technique gets the team members speaking and listening to one another (instead of talking and listening to the facilitator all the time) while they start to focus on positive moments in their lives. This leads to more interest in each other's sayings and thoughts and to a good atmosphere to work together on important topics.

- **Intervention: What else?**

    A further tool that is of use here is one of the most effective questions in coaching:

    And what else?

    When we are asked something, we typically try to give a short and quick answer, to move on and thus make good use of our resources. Only when we are asked again, do we think any deeper. The "what else?" question helps people to listen to themselves more closely, to find answers that are more valuable to them than those that they already know.

> **Practical Tip**
>
> Sample questions for each team member to answer at the opening of the retrospective:
>
> - What are you proud of achieving in the last two weeks? And what else (are you proud of)?
> - What have you done that has helped others? And what else (was helpful to others)?

We happily repeat this question in every retrospective. This creates a feeling of trust and encourages the team members to focus on functioning aspects between retrospectives. They begin to try, in the next retrospective, to have answers to this ever-recurring question. This effort then leads to finding and working on ever more of these functioning aspects, simply because you are concentrating on them.

7.2.2 Set Goals

Under such circumstances, a satisfactory result is rarely achieved.

Now that we have created a positive team atmosphere, we turn to the most important part of a retrospective. Setting the goal is sometimes difficult, and always necessary! Without a common goal, the team runs the risk of working in different directions or getting lost in the vast amount of topics.

To make a rapid focus possible, we usually ask a team only one of these questions, with the request that they formulate their common goal as one sentence within approximately 10–15 minutes.

When formulating a goal, describing how the desired future *should* look like, not how it should *not* look like, is important. The focus is thus on the presence of the desired, not the absence of the undesired. To maintain that focus, whenever we hear a negative formulation, we ask the question:

And what instead?

> **Practical Tip**
>
> Different ways of asking about a goal exist. Here are a few examples:
>
> - What goal do you want to reach?
> - What situation do you want to create?
> - What would be a large or small change?
> - Who will be the first person to notice that you have reached your goal? What would he or she notice that you are doing differently?
> - Assuming you've reached your goal, what would be different for you? What would be the impact of that?

7.2.2.1 Intervention: Turning Problems into Goals

Sometimes team members find it easier to talk about problems then about solutions. Problems are known; people have turned the problems in their heads around. All these thoughts want to get out—on paper first before the next step can be done. In that case, we use the following technique to find goals.

Take a flipchart and draw a line. On the left, write a heading called "Problems" (see Figure 7-1) and ask the team to write down current problems. Give only a short period of time, for example, three to five minutes, to reduce discussions about the problems.

Problems	Goals/Wishes

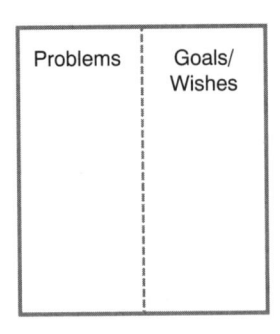

Figure 7-1 Turn problems into goals/wishes

After this is completed, write on the right-hand side "Goals/Wishes" and ask: "What would be achieved by removing these problems?" Now give more time to write that down. This is a form of asking: "What do you want to have instead?" Help the team to only write down positively formulated statements.

When the time is up, and the right-hand side is done, separate the goals from the problems by folding the paper on the line and carefully tearing it along the fold. As facilitator, we ask whether we may take the problems and promise that we'll take care of them, just in case the team would like their problems back. The team holds on to the wishes and goals and either chooses one or uses them to develop a common goal. This goal is then the focus of the remaining retrospective.

7.2.2.2 Intervention: Miracle Question

Only a miracle can help you now? The idea of that situation inspired Insoo Kim Berg to formulate the so-called "Miracle Question." The Miracle Question is a goal-setting question that is useful when a person or team simply does not know what a preferred future would look like. The precise language of the intervention might vary, but the basic wording is:

> *I am going to ask you a rather strange question [pause]. The strange question is this: [pause] After we talk, you will go back to your work (home, school) and you will do whatever you need to do the rest of today, such as taking care of the children, cooking dinner, watching TV, giving the children a bath, and so on. It will become time to go to bed. Everybody in your household is quiet, and you are sleeping in peace. In the middle of the night, a miracle happens and the problem that prompted you to talk to me today is solved! But because this happens while you are sleeping, you have no way of knowing that there was an overnight miracle that solved the problem [pause]. So, when you wake up tomorrow morning, what might be the small change that will make you say to yourself, "Wow, something must have happened—the problem is gone!" [6, p. 7]*

Let people tell everything in detail. Encourage more and more detail with the "And what else?" question. Focus also on what the involved people would do. Let people describe actions and possible reactions by others. Involve the whole team, other departments, supervisors, customers, and so on in the miracle. After hearing this question, many people see their desired future much clearer than before. Quite often evidence of concrete steps toward the realization of this miracle is hidden in the responses.

7.2.2.3 Goal Criteria

A clearly formulated goal is not only a significant piece of a retrospective but is also the basis for every form of successful communication. The goal (or goals) can only be achieved when it is clear. So, give this topic the appropriate priority and attention.

Please note, a goal is

- not a question, but a positive statement
- not an action, but a situation, described in detail, and with the relevant environment taken into account
- not a feeling, but something concrete
- within the team's sphere of influence
- practical and measurable

A helpful goal is comprehensible, meaningful, and can be implemented. Comprehensibility should be confirmed at the end of this phase. We will consider meaningfulness and applicability in the phases that follow.

7.2.3 Find Meaning

In 1997, Fredmund Malik wrote an article about "Motivation Through Meaning" in his *Malik on Management* newsletter. In the article, he mostly describes Viktor Frankl's teachings and indicates that they are the most important tasks in management. What goes for work in management is also valid for work with people in general, whatever the field in which it takes place.

Malik [7] writes, for example: "Thus, according to Frankl, people are motivated by meaning and the search for meaning. [...] When a person has found meaning, and as long as he is able to see a meaning in something, he is ready to do his absolute best and is ready to make sacrifices."

And further: "The search for meaning is the motivating force. However, meaning cannot be given to anyone. Each must find it for himself. You can, though, take meaning away from people; you can frustrate their search for meaning and thus destroy their most important source of power and their whole reason for being. Not to do so, but rather to provide opportunities for everyone to find meaning, is one of the most important tasks of leadership."

Mindful of Malik's observations, we work with the team to find the meaning of the common goal. The goal is often changed during this step to ensure that it really makes sense. As part of this, we consider direct and indirect consequences and influences.

7.2.3.1 Intervention: What For?

The most important question in finding meaning is:

What for?

The answer to that is sometimes hard to find, but after it has been found, you know the purpose of your goal.

Often, the question "Why?" is used for this purpose. We have found, however, that this question all too often leads to problems, as people try to find the reasons for problems and identify those responsible. That is why we recommend, as of now, to get rid of "Why?" and replace it with the question "What for?" "What for?" leads directly to the desired future and helps to understand and to find meaning.

> **Practical Tip**
> The following are questions that help to find meaning:
>
> - What do you want to reach your goal for?
> - What will be different then?
> - What impact would reaching your goal have for you? And what other impact?
> - What impact would it have for others? And what else?

In our work with teams, we have often noticed that the team's surroundings are insufficiently considered. We use the technique of circular questions to more actively build-in the external perspective.

7.2.3.2 Intervention: Circular Questions

Ask "around the corner" to find out what opportunities and risks people who are not here at this moment might see. Placing yourself in other minds and points of view expands your own range of possibilities and leads to new perspectives. For example:

- What do you think your boss would say about the impact achieving your goal would have?
- And what other impact would he expect?

This is important because the goal you have created should also be meaningful to other people involved. Otherwise, unexpected resistance could affect your success.

We also recommend updating your goal with new insights found at this step to recall them later.

7.2.4 Initiate Action

Now that you have created a meaningful goal, it is time to derive steps toward change. These steps can be quite small. For the implementation of the steps to be successful, it is usually important for the team to recognize that they already have the necessary competencies.

A popular intervention in the solution-focused approach is scaling.

7.2.4.1 Intervention: Scaling

Imagine a scale between zero and ten (see Figure 7-2), where ten represents the point at which the goal has been reached, and zero means the opposite.

0 ——————————————————— 10

Figure 7-2 Scale between zero and ten

Where are you at the moment (see Figure 7-3)?

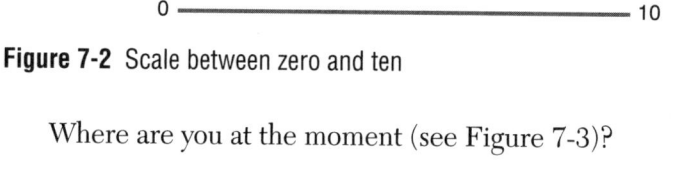

0 —————————✗————————— 10

Figure 7-3 Where are you at the moment?

Every team member is invited to take a position. This provides a moment to talk about signs of hope that reaching the goal is possible; that is, what works already. This strengthens the team's confidence and trust in its own abilities and skills to reach the goal. You can also usefully pick out positive differences. After all, it could have been "worse."

- What works already so that you are already at X rather than lower?
- How did you manage to be at...? What was your contribution?

Next, we use the scale to make once again the goal more concrete and visible.

- On this scale, where do you want to be so you can say that the situation has improved sufficiently (see Figure 7-4)?

0 —————✗—————📋——— 10

Figure 7-4 Where do you want to be?

Some people would really like to get to ten, but others feel they are already at the goal with a seven or an eight. It is often also recognized that bridging the gap to ten would require much more effort than is currently possible and that a smaller step is, therefore, sufficient.

Depending on how precisely the goal has been described in the previous step, you can again deepen the work on the goal.

- What will be different, when you reach ⊙?
- How will you recognize that you have reached ⊙?
- How will others notice that you have reached ⊙?
- Suppose you reached ⊙; what will you do differently?
- When do you want to be at ⊙?

To reach a goal, knowing concrete first steps toward the goal is helpful. Subsequent steps can change based on the result of the first step.

- Suppose you are one small step closer to the goal (see Figure 7-5), what will you have done to achieve this?
- And what else will you have done?

Figure 7-5 One small step closer to the goal

These questions should bring the small signs of progress back into focus. This is also about opening up a multitude of options and ideas so that the team can carry out concrete actions. We also record these steps in written form and thus give the team the possibility of keeping them in sight between retrospectives. Be alert to write down only positive formulation—otherwise ask the people for a positive formulation. Also, check whether the step is really a concrete first step or whether it is already a consequence of a step that you need to write down. Maybe enhance this list of steps with "when" and/or "who" if necessary, to create an actionable plan.

The simple structure of the scale offers three different focal points for the conversation:

- A realistic description of the desired future
- An enumeration of all of those things that are already going in the direction of the desired goal, including the successes already achieved
- The recognition of possible forward steps in the immediate future [8]

In several retrospectives, we carried out this scaling as a lineup of the team members in the room. Thus people involve their bodies when they stand in the situation and the desired future. This means that they can sense whether or not a position feels right. They are also better able to perceive the differences between the positions. Gut feeling comes into play here.

An added benefit is that team members' perspectives are very clear, and they have a chance to talk about their differences. Despite their different scaling of a situation, we have noticed that the team members' statements about what already works or what should be different are very similar. This understanding helps the team members to have more understanding for one another and thus reduces conflicts.

7.2.5 Check Results

So far so good. There is now a goal, it makes sense for all involved, and they know the first steps to achieving this goal. After all that work, we want to ensure that the results will be put into action. How certain are we that a person or team will actually realize their measures? Often little doubts must be uncovered, and we need to find solutions for dealing with them as well. Also, we want to increase the commitment of the team members.

We ask people to think briefly about their personal value out of the retrospective's results and then ask for a show of hands. Given the results, we might ask further:

- Assuming you would be a little more confident (for example, one value higher), what would be different then? What else will you need to be more confident?

These answers will lead the team to important insights and preconditions that need to be achieved before the main improvements can happen. Consider at least 10–15 minutes for this part as longer discussions could emerge again.

The confidence scale helps to

- check whether the results can actually be implemented
- discuss any remaining doubts and find ways to handle them successfully
- increase commitment to the agreement

7.2.6 A Brief, Solution-Focused Retrospective

Can you still remember the first questions from the opening? Add another question to that, and you have a short retrospective that you could use after a Standup meeting.

- What did you do yesterday that you were proud of?
- What did you do that helped others?
- Now that you know so much more, what would you do differently now?

To keep it short, accept the first answer to each question and don't add any follow-up questions. Depending on the size of the team and the available time, "what else?" questions would be a helpful extension.

Summary

In this chapter, we introduced the solution-focused approach and applied it to the design of retrospectives. For each step, we offered some interventions to use it in your practice. We learned for ourselves that those interventions work best when we fully believe in them. So, try those you feel comfortable with. Maybe it is something true and positive at the beginning of a meeting or the confidence scale at the end. Remember, small steps can lead to significant changes.

Retrospectives are starting points for change. Rarely does the change take place within the retrospective itself. With the team, take note of what aspects have a positive change after the retrospective. Focus on each small, positive variation.

You could easily build this into a daily Standup meeting. For example, ask the following (or a similar) question:

- What have you noticed since the last Standup that is bringing us closer to our common goal?

As already described, this focus on positive changes helps the team to stay motivated during their implementation of the steps.

Enjoy your experiments with the solution-focused approach and the celebration of your successes!

References

[1] Esther Derby and Diana Larsen. 2006. *Agile Retrospectives: Making Good Teams Great.* O'Reilly UK Ltd.

[2] Steve de Shazer. 1985. *Keys to Solution in Brief Therapy.* W. W. Norton & Company.

[3] Steve de Shazer. https://en.wikipedia.org/wiki/Steve_de_Shazer

[4] Barbara Fredrickson. 2009. *Positivity: Top-notch Research Reveals the Upward Spiral That Will Change Your Life.* Harmony.

[5] Marcial Losado and Emily Heaphy. 2004. "The Role of Positivity and Connectivity in the Performance of Business Teams." *American Behavioral Scientist*, Vol 47, Nr 6, p. 740–765.

[6] I.K. Berg and Y. Dolan. 2001. *Tales of Solutions: A Collection of Hope-Inspiring Stories*. New York: Norton.

[7] Fredmund Malik. 1997. *Malik on Management*. Nr 3/97, 5th Year, March 1997, p. 38ff.

[8] Chris Iverson, Evan George, and Harvey Ratner. 2012. *Brief Coaching—A Solution Focused Approach*. London: Taylor & Francis, p. 79.

[9] Viktor E. Frankl. 2006. *Man's Search for Meaning*. Beacon Press.

8

Distributed Retrospectives

The advance of globalization means that fewer and fewer teams work together in one place and are instead spread out over many places. This naturally creates a distance between team members. In the best of cases, these divided teams are all in the same time zone or in time zones with only very small time differences (one or two hours). However, ever more teams are distributed over the whole globe and whose working hours have absolutely no overlap. In addition to the time difference and physical distance between team members, there can also be distances created by culture, language, politics, or history. It goes without saying that this division has a large impact on the team and thus also on the carrying out of retrospectives. In this chapter, I discuss the challenges that arise from this situation and some ways of dealing with them.

8.1 Forms of Distributed Retrospectives

Each form of distributed retrospective presents its own challenges. To follow, I introduce the different forms and their specific challenges.

8.1.1 Multiple Distributed Teams

Multiple distributed teams are the variant with which I have had the most experience. These teams can be at the same physical location but are often distributed over several. In my experience, this form of organization has one serious disadvantage: Each individual team concentrates on itself and forgets to look past the end of its own nose.

In one of my last companies, we launched a new CMS (content management system) for a large client. This included a complete relaunch of its website. A total of three different teams were involved in this project:

- Our development team, at our company headquarters
- A development team at the client's site
- A further team, responsible for design, also at the client's site

Both our development team and the clients were working with an agile process. The only exception was the media design. As an agile coach, I was pulled into the project because of the various tensions between the teams. One of my observations was that while retrospectives were indeed being carried out, they were only ever local. Also, the results of each team's retrospectives were never shared with the other teams. How are you supposed to live a continuing improvement process when optimization is only carried out at the local level instead of the global? So, one of the first measures I took was to call a full-team retrospective. The retrospective would last a whole day and would be the first event in which all the team members took part at the same time. Aware of that fact, I focused on having the team members get to know one another better and introduce their perspectives to one another. So, I prepared activities suitable to that end. For many of the participants, this retrospective was a series of "a-ha" moments. Many of the things that had happened in the previous weeks and months appeared in a completely new light because the team now understood one another's perspectives. That day, we were able to clear away some misconceptions and lay the foundation for a successful project implementation. These joint retrospectives remained a part of the process and were carried out every two months. Six months later, the new system went online as per schedule.

In cases like the project I just described, when retrospectives are carried out, they are mostly local and do not directly involve all the teams. While this does lead to local improvements, the real problems in projects like this usually lie in the communication between and interaction of the teams. You should, therefore, attempt to hold joint retrospectives at regular intervals. These works best when everyone meets in the same place. Unfortunately, however, this is often impossible, and so you have to carry out a distributed retrospective. You need to be careful to carry out a few things for one of these retrospectives. I've prepared a checklist so that nothing gets left out:

- **Co-Facilitator**

    If it's next to impossible for two or more groups from different places to come together, find a co-facilitator at each location. This doesn't necessarily need to be an experienced facilitator but should be someone who knows the running order and will prepare the room appropriately.

- **Laptops**

    Every team member should have access to a laptop. This is the only way that you can all work together on a virtual board. The best practice is to have two people sit together per laptop. This makes the discussion more interactive and gives the participants less opportunity for doing other things with their laptops.

- **Projector**

    Have a projector in each of the rooms to display what is currently happening. This prevents a situation in which everyone just stares at his laptop.

- **Network**

    Without a network that works well, this retrospective just isn't going to happen. Make sure that it is working well before the retrospective. If you don't have access to a WLAN, you'll need to have sufficient cables and switches at hand.

- **Video Conference Tool**

    A decent video conference tool is also important. If possible, you should always be able to see the participants. The ability to read their body language is very important in a retrospective.

- **Online Board**

  Because not everybody can work together on a whiteboard, flipchart, or other wall space, you need to use a virtual board. I'll introduce some potential tools further on.

- **Preparation of the Online Board**

  You should appropriately prepare the online board, by showing the agenda, for example. You use an online board in the same way that you would use a real board or a flipchart.

  Because of the limitation to using the voice, having a skilled facilitator is even more important for retrospectives like these. The techniques described in Chapter 4 (stacking, paraphrasing, feeding back emotion, and so on) are particularly helpful here.

- **Added Preparation Time**

  I can tell you from experience that preparing for a distributed retrospective takes significantly more time than preparing for a normal one. So, make sure you have enough time planned out.

  If you stick to this checklist, you will, at the very least, lay the foundation for a potentially successful retrospective.

Practical Tip

There will always be teams that have to work without the tools described in the preceding. In most cases, they only have access to a normal teleconference connection. That means they have to do without visual communication tools. If you are in this position, I recommend that you share a document with all the participants via e-mail before the retrospective. This document should contain the following things:

- The agenda
- A description of the individual activities
- Placeholders, to carry out the (visual) activities locally

8.1.2 Teams with Singly Distributed Employees

Teams are often strengthened through the hiring of one or more freelancers, who most often work from home. At best, these team members come to the company offices every few weeks to work with the rest of the team. These are the best times to hold a retrospective because everyone is in the same place.

However, having individual team members come to the head office regularly is sometimes impossible. This is usually for one of two reasons:

- The cost of their travel is not covered by the company or is very high.
- The team member is immobile (because of a physical handicap, for example).

The major disadvantage of this situation is that these individual team members are often unintentionally overlooked and not seen as part of the team. This is usually because a suitable communication structure is not available or is not used. The individually distributed team members are only communicated with when it is absolutely necessary, as at daily Standups, for example. And that's completely natural. Starting a conversation with someone is much easier when he or she is sitting next to or across from you, than when you have to use a special tool. Meeting an external team member at the coffee machine and having a chat about the weekend is also impossible.

Not long ago, I stumbled across a brilliant solution to this problem. Double Robotics [1] is a company that builds robots that make it possible for me to be in a place without having to travel there myself. To do this, the company uses an iPad placed on a moveable robot. The iPad runs a special app that allows me to move the robot to wherever I like. At the same time, the other team members can see me on the iPad's screen and can thus keep in contact with me. It's really a mobile video conference system. So, Double Robotics makes it possible for me to take part in all the team's meetings. I can even be there for the chat around the coffee machine. The battery lasts for 8 hours so I can spend a full workday with the rest of the team. This solution is relatively cheap when you consider the advantages to be had.

If you don't have access to such brilliant solutions and still have to run retrospectives in which one or more of the team is alone at their home office, you need to consider the following things covered in the following sections.

8.1.2.1 Pairing

Make sure that each external team member is allocated a partner in the on-site team for the duration of the retrospective. This ensures that each external team member is well integrated into the retrospective and that his voice is heard.

8.1.2.2 Videoconference

As in retrospectives with multiple distributed teams, use a video conferencing tool here. The external team member needs to be able to see the team and vice versa. This also prevents his presence from being lost in the general hurly-burly of a retrospective.

8.1.2.3 Online Board

If even only one team member is external, you should use an online board. This ensures that the external team member can see all the results of the work and can contribute to it himself.

In this team structure (teams with individual team members), the facilitator's most important task is to make sure that the external team member is not forgotten or ignored, but well integrated. That isn't always an easy job for the facilitator. However, if you hold to the preceding points, you will create a good foundation that will turn even this kind of retrospective into a success. In my view, pairing is the most important brick in that foundation.

8.1.3 Scattered Teams

Recently, more and more teams exist whose members all sit at home in their own workspaces instead of together in a large office. To communicate with one another, they use all the different tools that are available online. An example of this is from the U.S. company Automattic [2], which is responsible for WordPress and Gravatar, among other solutions. Automattic is a very good example of how you can dispense with emails and still communicate well with one another. Employees at Automattic communicate primarily with WordPress blogs that are set up with the P2 theme [3]. These blogs make possible the exchange of information and ideas in real time and prevent important information from disappearing in an e-mail inbox. They also use tools like Skype or AIM clients. Group discussions mainly happen via IRC (Internet Relay Chat), one of the oldest ways of conversing online.

You can safely assume that such organizations know how to communicate within distributed systems. Of course, this also applies to distributed retrospectives. Still, the following is a short checklist of what to keep in mind in such a case.

8.1.3.1 The Facilitator

The identity of the facilitator must be clearly determined. As a rule, it is the person who has called the retrospective. This ensures that there is someone to lead the retrospective and to help the team get meaningful results. The facilitator should also bring a certain experience because these retrospectives are certainly among the most difficult.

8.1.3.2 Interactive Activities

The danger always exists in these distributed retrospectives that someone will "drift off," or cease to be mentally present. That is why it is important to make sure that all the activities you choose have an interactive component, in which the participants have to do something. When dealing with scattered teams, avoid activities that are primarily spoken. After a certain number of people are present, spoken activities rapidly become unproductive.

8.1.3.3 Videoconference

It goes without saying that you need a video conference tool. Holding a distributed retrospective in purely auditory form is very difficult.

These points certainly do not guarantee successful, distributed retrospectives, but they do provide a base. In the next section, I give you a few general tips for leading distributed retrospectives to a successful outcome.

8.1.3.4 Online Board

Of course, in a retrospective like this, you must have an online board as the primary form of visual communication. Because nobody is sitting in a room with another team member, you need a virtual whiteboard.

8.2 The Right Tools

Purely auditory retrospectives, those based solely on what is said and heard, are sub-optimal even in on-site retrospectives. They are even more difficult in distributed retrospectives. That is why I believe that the most important tool for distributed retrospectives is a visualization tool. You can use either graphic templates that are sent to the participants beforehand and used during the retrospective or use an online tool that allows the participants to interact with one another visually. In my view, the use of visual tools is much more effective at keeping the participants in line.

> **Practical Tip**
> Whichever tool you choose, make sure you try it out first. Only when you know your tool well can you use it effectively in a retrospective.

Distributed retrospectives are more successful when the participants can see each other. Happily, in today's world of Skype and Google Hangout, this is ever easier to achieve. Of course, the best tools are those that combine both elements. In the next section, I introduce a few tools that you can use in distributed retrospectives. Of course, many more tools are also available online, including a lot for which you have to pay. It is also worth noting that the tools I describe below might no longer be available in the coming months or years. Still, I would like to introduce three options that I have grown to love.

8.2.1 Web Whiteboard

As the name suggests, the Web Whiteboard tool is an online whiteboard [4] that offers all the functions of real whiteboards:

- Hang up and move self-stick notes
- Draw
- Write

So, it's a good substitute if you aren't all sitting together in the same room. A web whiteboard can be simply shared using a link. Everyone who has the link can work on the whiteboard. Whiteboards can also be password protected. You can use a web whiteboard the way that you would use a normal one: for example, to write up the agenda or hang up self-stick notes from a round of brainstorming. It is thus useful at every stage of a retrospective. This tool does have a few disadvantages:

- You need a Google account to be able to protect it with a password. Additionally, this function is set to become a premium function in the future and will thus carry a charge for use.
- When using Web Whiteboard, you need a second tool to speak to each other, either a teleconference connection or a tool like Skype.

Despite these disadvantages, Web Whiteboard has often proven to be a tool that is effective and easy to use. Because it's a web application, no installation is required. It isn't cluttered and offers everything you need for a retrospective.

8.2.2 Stormz Hangout

Stormz Hangout [5] is based on Google Hangouts and thus has a lot built in: video conferencing, chat, desktop sharing, and more. In addition to the basic functions, the application provides a framework that can lead you and your participants through a retrospective. This tool is currently free.

When you create a new retrospective, you're first asked for the name and a more precise description of the content. The precise description is optional. You can then invite the participants to the retrospective, regardless of whether they have a Google account or not. As soon as all the participants are present, the actual retrospective starts. The five steps are:

1. Enter all the events from the last iteration (positive as well as negative) on virtual cards. For each event, a card is created that is visible to all the participants.
2. Look at the cards and discuss them. You can also use this step to create clusters and organize the cards appropriately.
3. You can distribute a virtual $100 among the cards to choose the most important topics.
4. You each get a card. The task is to write a possible improvement for the topic shown on the card.
5. This ends the standardized process, but you can add on as many further steps as you like. Edit each of these steps to fit your current situation.

However, this tool also has a few disadvantages:

- It completely ignores the Set the Stage and Generate Insights. You can do this differently, of course, but Stormz Hangout doesn't provide support.
- You cannot assign a value to individual improvements on the cards. You can only assign a value to a whole card. If there is more than one improvement on a card, you have to find another way to value each of them, such as attaching a comment to the card.

The process is quite rigid and can only be adapted to a certain extent. Despite these disadvantages, it is an interesting tool for leading a distributed retrospective. However, I believe it is too inflexible for long term, regular use.

8.2.3 Lino

The last tool in the bundle that I want to introduce is Lino. Lino is a kind of virtual corkboard for pinning up self-stick notes, photos, videos, and so on. These are then visible to everyone who has the board's URL. Lino, like Web Whiteboard, has no standardized process so you can use it however you want—to post the agenda, for example, or to collect ideas. Compared to the other tools, though, Lino has one decisive disadvantage: You can't protect your board very easily. You can label it "private," but this makes it invisible to the other participants. Especially in larger companies, this is a reason why it couldn't be used. You can always delete the board after the retrospective, but then you lose your results. Despite this disadvantage, Lino is a simple and effective tool for visually supporting a retrospective.

8.3 General Tips for Distributed Retrospectives

To follow, I want to give a few general tips for leading distributed (and sometimes also local) retrospectives. They are applicable in all the cases described earlier.

8.3.1 Keep It Short

Even if you're a great facilitator, keeping a virtual retrospective interesting over a longer period of time will be an effort. If you're not all sitting in the same room, keeping the energy level up for the duration is very difficult. That is why a distributed retrospective should be as short as possible. You will seldom be able to keep the participants in line for longer than an hour. If you're planning a longer retrospective, having all the team members together in one place makes more sense.

8.3.2 Stay within the Timeframe

When you share the agenda with the participants, include exact times for the individual activities. You should then keep to those times during the actual retrospective. This ensures that you'll be able to stop punctually after an hour.

8.3.3 Use Stacking

In a distributed retrospective in which the participants can only hear each other, it is extremely important to make sure that everyone gets a chance to speak and that no one is left out. A good tool to ensure this is the stacking technique I described in Chapter 4.

8.3.4 Prepare the Participants

Share the topic of the retrospective with the participants in advance, especially when they will be considering a special topic. This enables the participants to prepare themselves. Retrospectives are thus made more effective, and you are more likely to be able to stay within your timeframe.

8.3.5 Use Communication Tools Effectively

Become an expert in all the communication tools that are available to you in your organization. Professional tools are often available, especially in larger organizations. Some examples are Cisco Conference systems, digital whiteboards (such as from 3M), online collaboration software (Basecamp), and online conference tools (WebEx or GoTo Meeting). Get to know all the useful functions of these tools so that you can use them quickly and effectively in your retrospectives.

8.3.6 Meet Regularly

Despite distribution, having teams meet regularly makes sense. An annual meeting can be perfectly sufficient. It is a simple fact that true human connection can only happen when people meet face to face. You'll also be able to hold better retrospectives with people with whom you have partied.

Summary

Nothing beats a collocated team. But the reality is that you have to accept that more and more distributed teams are out there. This means facilitators have to find ways to cope with this setup. In this chapter, I described the different forms of distributed teams and what to keep in mind for each of them. Additionally, I listed some tools that you can use in a distributed setup:

- Web Whiteboard
- Stormz Hangout
- Lino

All of them are free, so you don't have to pay a dime. Of course, even more are out there, so keep your eyes open. If you want to use more professional tools that are specially created for agile retrospectives, have a look at the following tools:

- Retrium [6]
- Sensei [7]

Both of them are great tools.

This chapter finished with some general tips on how to facilitate distributed agile retrospectives. Now you are well prepared to start with your own distributed challenge.

References

[1] Double Robotics Company Website. 2017. https://www.doublerobotics.com/

[2] Automattic Company Website. 2017. https://automattic.com/

[3] P2 WordPress Theme. 2017. https://p2theme.com/

[4] Web Whiteboard Website. 2017. https://www.webwhiteboard.com/

[5] Stormz Hangout Website. 2017. http://stormzhangout.com/

[6] Retrium Website. 2017. http://www.retrium.com/

[7] Sensei Website. 2017. https://www.senseitool.com

9

Alternative Approaches

This chapter articulates some alternative approaches to and ways of thinking about retrospectives. These don't conform strictly to the phase model of standard retrospectives and are sometimes completely different. The ideas in this chapter are designed to help you make retrospectives even more interesting.

9.1 Work Retrospectives

At the beginning of 2013, I stumbled across a blog post by Yves Hanoulle, in which he described a special form of retrospective: the work retrospective. Like many other retrospective facilitators, he has often met teams that had no further interest in doing retrospectives. In most cases, these teams explained the reason for their lack of interest as follows:

- Nothing ever really changes.
- Why is it always just us that must change?
- We're never given the time to implement our new ideas.

The basic idea behind the work retrospective is to tackle these reasons in one retrospective.

9.1.1 Set the Stage

The Set the Stage phase is carried out just as it is in every other retrospective. All the activities that you can use in phase one in other retrospectives will work here. Yves' favorite activity (at the beginning of 2013) is called "Check-In." It goes like this:

- Whoever's turn it is says: "I am [one or more of the following: mad, sad, glad, or afraid]." If he wants to, he can also give a short explanation of why he feels that way. However, the person is also allowed to say "Pass" and add nothing more. Here's an example: "I am mad because Hans came late to the retrospective, again."
- After he has finished, the person says: "I'm here."
- Everybody else says: "Welcome."

You can find more information about this activity on Jim and Michelle McCarthy's blog [1].

9.1.2 Gather Data

In a normal retrospective, the Gather Data phase is used to gather data from the preceding weeks. A work retrospective takes a different approach. The participants are given self-stick notes and asked to write down two actions that, in their view, need to be addressed and can be completed within an hour. They get five minutes to write, and then each person briefly presents his ideas. Your job is to make sure that everyone gets a turn and presents a maximum of two ideas.

Finally, everyone finds a partner and a task that they would like to work on together. Some people find their partner first and then their task. Some people do it the other way around. Either way works.

9.1.3 Work Phase

Now comes the actual "work" phase of the work retrospective. Each pair gets exactly one hour in which to work on their task. An hour is a fairly short space of time, but the individual teams have to try to complete their task in small steps. Whatever the results look like after the hour is up, the participants all gather together to present their results. Each pair gets a maximum of five minutes in which to present.

9.1.4 Experiences

I'd like to quote Yves' own experience to you:

On most teams, there are people who hate this. In lots of cases, these are also the people that complain most that they never get the time to do anything. I ignore them in this exercise. The rules are the same for everyone. (That's why I use lots of different retrospective formats.)

Usually, there are about the half of the teams that have been able to do something useful. And when this happens, everyone in the team is taught it's possible. And this is not me convincing them, their team has done it.

I once had a team complaining for 3 months that the homepage of their website was unstable because of unstable web-services. In 1 hour, 1 pair had identified +60 calls to web-services, and they had fixed 40 of them. The updated was life in the hour. The next day, one of the developers, took the time to fix the other 20. We won that extra hour back in the same week, as our testers lost less time.

Every time there is a pair that is not ready for the demo. They keep working while their colleagues are demoing. I make it very clear that they won't be able to demo. That usually stops them from working. I do this as they now pay attention to their teammates that were able to split into smaller tasks.

Sometimes there is also a pair cheating, and they show something they have been working on secretly. I don't say anything about that. At least the secret project is now out. Remember, it's not a competition. It's about solving a problem [2].

I'm a big fan of this kind of retrospective. It certainly isn't one that you can carry out often, but it is a retrospective in which people can learn a lot. When it goes well, the team members learn that it's possible to get moving in a short amount of time. When it goes even better, you achieve something very significant for the team in a short time. What usually gets done in work retrospectives are small things that keep getting put off and for which you finally make the time. An additional benefit is that crossing something off your to-do list always feels good. Give this retrospective a try. I'd love to hear your feedback.

Practical Tip

The very time to carry out a work retrospective is when it seems that you don't have the time. Doing this enables you to implement at least a few small improvements. These could well have a larger impact than you might think.

9.2 Fortune Cookie Retrospectives

A few years ago, I came across a funny idea from an agile coach in the USA. Adam Weisbart had discovered that the best retrospectives in which he took part all had two things in common:

- Questions that make you think
- Something to eat

He concluded that a good retrospective should have these two things as their center point. As a big fan of Chinese food, he came up with the idea of a fortune cookie retrospective.

You know fortune cookies, those tasty little cookies that are presented as a dessert in practically every Chinese restaurant. The whole point of fortune cookies, of course, is that they have inside them a slip of paper with your "fortune." For instance, "great changes are ahead" or "soon you will experience a windfall." Instead of these meaningless statements, Adams' cookies contain questions created for the team. These questions are designed to get the team thinking. What I particularly like about his questions is their focus on the team itself. Teams often neglect to consider their own behavior and only ever see problems on the outside.

A fortune cookie retrospective goes like this:

- Each participant gets a fortune cookie.
- After this, the participants take turns to open their cookie, read the question, and then come up with an answer. You can also give the participants five minutes in which to get their answers down on paper.
- The facilitator's task is to ask further questions designed to find out more or to ask other participants for their opinions.

The results of this round of questioning can be used during the rest of the retrospective, so I also recommend that the participants write their answers down on self-stick notes and then display these on a whiteboard. As each participant posts his idea, he explains the thinking behind his answer.

This kind of retrospective makes a nice change when you want to do something very different with your team. I have carried out several fortune cookie retrospectives, and each time the participants had a lot of fun. By the way, you can order the cookies online from Adam Weisbart [3]. The delivery cost is quite high, but I haven't yet found a cheaper way to get my hands on the right cookies. If you're feeling inspired, you can always make your own [4].

9.3 Powerful Questions

Powerful questions are actually a coaching tool. These are open questions that aren't simply looking for an answer but are designed to get people to reconsider old habits, positions, or assumptions. Generally, you can say that questions that ask *why, what,* or *how* are more powerful than questions that ask *who, when,* or *where*. The least powerful questions are those that begin with *whose*, or that solicit a simple yes or no answer. So you could say that powerful questions are those that encourage an extensive answer. Not for nothing are most small children experts at the question: why?

The trick to asking a powerful question is not to take the easy way out by asking a weak question, which very often leads to short and simple answers and doesn't get you any further. Another common mistake is to ask a *why* question that tries to pin the blame for something on someone. Far from opening up a constructive discussion, this just closes people off and makes them defensive.

> **Example**
> **Situation:** A team member is going on about something that happened months before.
> **Weak Question:** Why are we still talking about this topic? (Implying: "Cut it out!")
> **Powerful Question:** What can we learn from that?

Powerful questions can be used during a retrospective and can also be a very good way of getting them started. Here are a few examples of powerful questions that you can use to kick-start your retrospectives:

- What can we afford to leave out?
- What is something that already works and that you can build on?
- What would your hero say?

- What's today's theme tune?
- What's not being said?
- What is giving the most value?
- What would a wise person whisper in your ear?
- What's the worst that can happen?
- How can we minimize the risks?
- How is our team going to be perceived from the outside?
- How can we create a learning space?
- How often have we left our most pressing problem to one side?

None of the preceding questions can be answered without considerable thought. The purpose of some of the questions doesn't even seem clear initially. All of these questions are designed to tempt a team or an individual off the usual, well-trodden path and onto a new road. That is what makes them so well suited to helping develop new ideas in a retrospective.

You can also use powerful questions in the Gather Data phase. For example, you might ask the question, "What's the worst thing that can happen at this moment?" You give each of the participants self-stick notes and get them to collect answers to this question. The facilitator then reads out the answers and asks questions to get more information if necessary. Together, you all decide on the three worst things that could happen and that you want to deal with proactively. You then move into the Generate Insights phase and form three groups, with each group taking one of the answers and working to find possible causes. In the end, each group presents its results so that, in the Define Experiments phase, the whole team can look for ways to prevent the worst from happening.

Based on the content of the question and the way it is asked, you can develop thoroughly different retrospectives. The preceding example was a retrospective based on the worst things that could happen to the project team. The end results are measures that can be undertaken proactively. If, instead, you had chosen the question "What is something that already works and that you can build on?" you would have moved the retrospective in a completely different direction.

In that case, participants would have looked for good things that could be made better. So powerful questions are a good tool for making retrospectives a little different and, sometimes, also for shaking up existing structures and processes.

Summary

Trying out new retrospective formats and leaving the standard format behind can sometimes be refreshing. It opens up new perspectives and can help teams become unstuck. In this chapter, you learned about the work retrospective, which uses the time of the retrospective to get the team's hands dirty and solve something immediately—no more excuses that no one has the time.

The Fortune Cookie retrospective combines food and thoughtful questions, and the knowledge of powerful questions will always help you as facilitator to ask the right questions.

References

[1] Jim McCarthy and Emily McCarthy. 2010. *Check In*. https://liveingreatness.com/core-protocols/check-in/

[2] Yves Hanoulle. 2013. *Work Retrospectives*. http://www.hanoulle.be/2013/03/work-retrospective/

[3] Adam Weisbart. 2011. *Retrospective Cookies*. https://weisbart.com/cookies

[4] allrecipes. *Fortune Cookies recipe*. http://allrecipes.com/recipe/9684/fortune-cookies-i/

10

Typical Problems and Pitfalls

As with everything in life, retrospectives do have a few typical problems and pitfalls for which you should be prepared. These things can make your life very difficult indeed and have a decisive influence on the success of a retrospective. In this chapter, I'll introduce some of these problems and pitfalls, as well as some possible solutions.

10.1 Poor Preparation

Some people treat retrospectives as they do any other meeting. That is, it's enough to send out an invitation, sit down in the room and get started. Some other people believe that all you need to carry out a retrospective is a simple question, something like: "What do you want to do better in the next iteration?" As you've seen over the course of this book, that's clearly rubbish. A retrospective has very little in common with a meeting. A retrospective is much more of a workshop, which needs to be well prepared. If you've had some experience as a retrospective facilitator, you can occasionally pull a retrospective out of your hat without much preparation. But that's the exception, not the rule. If you want the best possible results from a retrospective, you need to invest a certain amount of time in preparation. Good preparation is half the battle. You can tell straight away whether or not a facilitator is well prepared and excited about working with the team to get good results. Of course, that has a corresponding effect on the participants. As a participant, you immediately feel better if the room has been carefully prepared. A well-prepared room has an energy all of its own. It's also important to note that most professionals seldom take part in well-thought-out and carefully prepared workshops. Don't ever underestimate the first impression.

In short, a poorly prepared retrospective doesn't just have a negative effect on the team, it has a negative effect on you, too. A poorly prepared retrospective will also lower the participants' opinions of retrospectives in general and will make it much more difficult to get people to participate again. Remember: you will only get the best out of retrospectives if you repeat them at short and regular intervals.

10.2 A Lot of Discussions but No Results

You know those endless meetings that have no clear results. The whole meeting is spent discussing and discussing until you're suddenly out of time. The result is that, while you might have had some valuable discussion, you haven't created any tangible results and so it has been of no help to anyone. The same can happen in retrospectives. Here are some reasons for retrospectives that end with no results:

- Conflicting opinions
- Indecision
- The lack of a clear time frame

10.2.1 *Conflicting Opinions*

A few months ago, I led a project retrospective that was intended to shed some light on the last year of the project. The retrospective went well until we came to the penultimate phase: Define Next Experiments. After a successful brainstorming, we ran into trouble while trying to agree on the next steps. You should know that a conflict had been brewing in this team for some time. One of the team members didn't agree with the approach that had been taken up to this point and wanted to arrange the team differently. This wasn't about making a small change, but about restructuring the team from the ground up. It quickly became clear that there were two people in the team who had strongly conflicting opinions: the team leader, who wanted to keep the current model, and a person who had only recently joined the team. After I had listened to them both for a while and the discussion had become ever more circular, I stopped them. Next, I restated the two conflicting opinions, as I had understood them. Finally, I suggested that they try out both options, one after another, for a predetermined period of time. They could then meet again to assess which had worked better. Both parties agreed to this, and we were able to end the retrospective with success.

> **Practical Tip**
>
> As a facilitator, if you notice that two completely contradictory positions have developed and the team isn't able to agree, you need to stop the discussion. The first step is to re-state the two positions, as you have understood them. Then you look for anything they might have in common. They will actually often have a lot more in common than you might think. A team can choose it next steps on the basis of this common ground.

If you can't get any agreement, suggest the approach described in the nearby Practical Tip. Doing this makes it clear to all the participants that none of them can say with certainty that his model or suggested solution is best. You can only say that after it has been tried. In the end, everything is just an experiment to test a hypothesis. Both of the solutions suggested are tested for a predetermined period of time. After both have been tried, you meet again to compare the results. You can then define the next steps based on these results. The possibility also exists that neither of the options worked well and that you have to find a completely new approach.

In this way, everyone gets a chance to try out their solution and show that their variant is the best. Everyone feels that they have been listened to and that has an excellent effect on future teamwork.

10.2.2 Indecision

You know them—those dysfunctional meetings that go around in circles and never produce clear results. If decisions are made, they're not possible to implement without further work and seem more like an alibi than a concrete measure. You see these meetings most often in companies that have suffered a complete loss of confidence. In my experience, this is more likely in larger companies.

> **Practical Tip**
>
> One of a facilitator's tasks is to prevent this kind of indecision-filled situations from developing. It is extremely important that you make sure that you have planned in enough time for the decision-making process; that is, for the Define Next Experiments and Hypotheses phase.

I have often seen how time has suddenly run out and a retrospective has to be stopped before it has produced any results. You also have to make sure that the time set aside for decision-making is used well. If a discussion is starting to go around in circles, you need to step in and paraphrase what has already been said. If it's possible, see if you can extract some implementable measures. Sometimes, it makes sense to note explicitly that all the decisions taken under consideration are only experiments. This can help to reduce anxiety around taking a decision. Additionally, the use of hypotheses can help to define meaningful experiments and, simultaneously, create a basis for examining, in the next retrospective, whether or not they had a tangible effect. Last, but not least, you need to ensure that each experiment has been assigned a latest start date and someone to carry it out.

10.2.3 Lack of a Clear Time Frame

In my opinion, having clear time frames for each of the phases of a retrospective is one of the most significant factors that influences the success of a retrospective. It follows that one of a facilitator's most important tasks is making sure that the participants keep to those time frames. This is especially important during short retrospectives because you will otherwise have no chance of getting results. If you keep going over the time limit, you will have no time left at the end in which to define the next experiments. Then you will end up with either wooly results, or no results at all, so keep strictly to your agenda. This also gives the participants the impression that you run retrospectives in an efficient and targeted way. They will come to value the fact that your retrospectives nip pointless discussions in the bud and lead to results.

> **Practical Tip**
>
> In some situations you can let a discussion continue. As you gain experience as a facilitator, you begin to get a feeling for which discussions are moving you forward and which are counterproductive or starting to go round in circles. If a discussion is moving you forward, you can let it run, but then make sure that you adjust the time allotted for the remaining phases appropriately. My experience has been that this works well in longer retrospectives because you have relatively a lot of room to be flexible. The shorter the retrospective, the more difficult this is. In one-hour retrospectives, I keep very strictly to the time frames.

The better you can keep your retrospective aligned with the agenda you've prepared beforehand, the fewer retrospectives you will have that end without results.

> **Practical Tip**
> So that keeping to the allotted times isn't stressful, make sure to keep letting the team know how much time is left in each phase. This motivates participants to come to the point and end discussions that are going around in circles.

10.3 Too Many Results

Teams doing a retrospective for the first time usually tend to saddle themselves with too much to do. By the end of the retrospective, they have ten or more suggestions for what they want to get to work on in the coming weeks, which makes it hard to choose. At the same time, a team like that is full of fire and would ideally like to change the whole world. There are three main problems with this.

First, you always need to be very careful when making changes. The more you want to change and the bigger the change, the higher the resistance within the system. Implementing all of these changes would thus be exponentially more difficult. Also, the old processes and approaches can't be laid aside all that easily, even if it does seem that a change is bearing fruit. Many changes are only superficial and don't last in the long run because the old patterns of operation re-assert themselves after a while. If you try to implement too many changes at once, you will necessarily be investing too little time in anchoring the new change deeply into the system.

Another problem is simply time. In most cases, a team is working on a project and can't invest all of their time in making the changes. You'd have a hard time explaining to the customer and other interest groups why you're spending the bulk of your time implementing the various changes. So, you need to limit yourself to a small number of changes.

Finally, as you've already seen in section 1.3, "The Retrospective Phase Model," in Chapter 1, tying all changes and experiments to hypotheses makes sense. The hypothesis can help you find out, in the next retrospective, whether or not the measures had the desired effect. If you do too many things at once, figuring out which measure is responsible for which effect is almost impossible. If I take five different medicines to cure my cold, I can't say in the end which one actually made me feel better. So, if you want to know which measures are responsible for which effects, you have to, as in a good scientific experiment, reduce the number of possible variables. That is the only way to establish a goal-oriented improvement process.

> **Practical Tip**
>
> The facilitator's task is to help the team reduce the number of experiments as much as possible. The best thing is to agree on one experiment. Any more than three experiments is definitely too much and will only lead to frustration in the long run. One way in which to agree on a single experiment is to use Dot Voting I already introduced in Chapter 1, "Retrospectives 101."

10.4 Disinterest in (Further) Improvement

You can see a marked disinterest in further improvements in some teams. They seem to have lost any and all motivation to do retrospectives, and even getting them to work up meaningful results is an effort. I don't offer up a general solution to this problem, because it is always so dependent on the context of the situation. A situation like this is usually caused by one of the three following things:

- The improvements chosen in previous retrospectives were never implemented.
- The improvements chosen had no effect: nothing changed.
- The team didn't get enough time to work on the chosen improvements.

10.4.1 Improvements Were Never Implemented

Most of the time, the reason that improvements aren't implemented is that they simply get lost in day-to-day business. It also doesn't help to set deadlines and assign people tasks if the improvements are no longer visible to anyone. This means that in the next retrospective, no one talks about the improvements that were chosen last time. The end result for the team is frustration.

A good retrospective needs an appropriate evaluation (see section 4.4) The results should be evaluated and posted in the team room. Results that are displayed on wikis or distributed by e-mail have been forgotten by the following day. If the team uses a board on which all of their tasks are displayed (the Sprint backlog in Scrum), then the improvements chosen in the retrospective should be displayed there. That is the only way to ensure that the team doesn't lose sight of them.

> **Practical Tip**
> The tasks from the last retrospective are an integral part of the current retrospective. As a rule, defining new improvements if the old ones haven't yet been implemented doesn't make any sense.

10.4.2 Improvements Have No Effect

Many teams in the first months of a continuous improvement process celebrate each and every success. The beginning is the easiest time to see and implement potential improvements. However, after these "low-hanging fruits" have been harvested, the process grinds to a halt, and it seems you can't get moving.

The first thing to understand is that every improvement, every measure, that is chosen in a retrospective remains nothing more than an experiment. In the world of work, you are most often dealing with complex, adaptive systems whose behavior can only be partially predicted. So you really can't know in advance whether or not you will get the effect you have imagined. That is why it is also important that you equip each of your experiments with a hypothesis. That way you can check, in the next retrospective, whether or not the measure (the experiment) from the last retrospective had the desired effect. If they haven't, you can use the current retrospective to define a new experiment. Continue to do so until you are satisfied with the effect and have reached your goal. A side effect of this approach is that your retrospectives always have clear goals and are thus, in yet another way, valuable meetings. Additionally, it's helpful if the team members are familiar with system thinking and complexity thinking (see Chapter 6) so as to better understand how to influence the system in which they work.

10.4.3 The Team Was Not Given Enough Time

People often complain that they don't get enough time in their daily work to implement the experiments (improvements). Other tasks take priority, and nobody gets a chance to change anything really.

A good thing to try in this situation is the work retrospective (see section 9.1 "Work Retrospectives," in Chapter 9). This can help demonstrate that even small improvements contribute to a continuing improvement process.

10.5 Focus on the Negative

Not long ago, I took part in a retrospective that began with the following sentence: "So, let's collect all the things that went badly in the last iteration." No introduction, just that sentence. The team used the rest of the retrospective to discuss all the negative things that had caused them problems in the preceding weeks. The worst part was that every one of that team's retrospectives began with that same sentence. You can well imagine how difficult it would be to create a positive atmosphere in that situation.

Never mind that looking at the negative results should only be a very small part of a retrospective. Focusing on solving problems is good. Unfortunately, that all too often leads to concentrating on mistakes and failures.

A continuing improvement process is an evolutionary process. That does mean that things that don't work are dropped, but also, and much more importantly that things that work well are kept and further developed. Giraffes haven't been running around with long necks since day one. The long necks developed little by little. If evolution had stopped at a mid-length neck, there wouldn't be any giraffes alive today.

You want to achieve in retrospectives what evolution has with the giraffe's neck. A specific place exists in many retrospective activities for all the good things that happen. Take, for example, the simple activity called "Start, Stop, Continue." The Continue field is intended for all the things that you want to keep because they have worked well in the preceding weeks. You can also use the Glad field in the "Sad, Mad, Glad" activity, in which the team collects all the things that feel positive. A good facilitator makes sure that these positive things aren't lost over the course of the retrospective. Many people make the mistake of more or less ignoring the collection of positive things and working only with the other data during a retrospective. Additionally, positive results should be appropriately celebrated. They serve the purpose of showing the team that many things have gone well. This can inject an extra dose of energy into a retrospective that makes for even better results.

10.6 Focus on Factual Topics

It's normal for teams that are just starting to do retrospectives to focus first on "tangible" things. For one thing, these are often much easier to solve (a continuous integration server, for example, can be set up very quickly) and, for another, it gives you the feeling of being able to get things moving. In the beginning, then, factual topics are not unusual and are perfectly normal. After a certain point, though, they are no longer enough. When people work together in a team, it is necessarily going to get "human." I know of very few teams in which there are absolutely no conflicts. A team can also start to crack where it meets the outside world. However, there are also more positive things in this area. Each team member brings a potential that should not be underestimated but positively developed, but that is only possible when team members are open and work with each other to further develop. So you can't get around discussing these topics, which are also a part of a continuing improvement process. But what do you do if a team refuses to work on the more soft topics of a team, like conflicts?

The hard truth is that no simple solution exists to create a safe and open environment and certainly no patented method. That is because the causes of this problem are extremely dependent on the context of the situation and the people involved. Everyone is different. I have two children, who grew up in the same environment, who have the same rules and have to suffer the same approach to childrearing. Despite that, they are fundamentally different. Why should it be any different in a company or team?

From my point of view, the main causes of the problem I just described are the people involved and the culture of the company. The interplay of these two things has an added effect. If I'm dealing with a company culture that has been rigidly hierarchical, in which the boss or the management rule through fear and pressure, and in which everyone is used to simply obeying orders, I can't expect the employees to be open with each other. Companies like that often run on the cover your ass (CYA) maxim: Don't take any risks or make any changes unless you can be sure that someone else will get the blame if it doesn't work. It's always someone else's fault. If you're dealing with a company like that, you're holding bad cards. However, if management supports improving such a culture, put everything into implementing a process of change.

The highest priority, in this case, is to create an environment for the employees in which they feel comfortable and can be open; an environment of self-direction and mutual trust; an environment in which all decisions are made transparently, and so on. Retrospectives can certainly help, but providing intensive coaching is a more important step. Get an expert into the building to focus on and support the company in the rarely simple task of changing its culture. If you can establish such a positive environment in your company, then the employees will naturally be more open. However, you do need to accept that some employees will leave the company because they don't feel comfortable in the new culture.

If you have the good fortune to work in an open and trusting company culture, but still have the problem I described earlier, the reason is usually that the employees are afraid to be open. They are afraid to let themselves be exposed and vulnerable. One of a facilitator's most important tasks is to recognize this and to create a safe and comfortable atmosphere in a retrospective. That starts with preparing the room. A 10 pound box of gummy bears can work wonders. It's amazing how the simple presence of something to eat instantly loosens up the atmosphere. You lay the foundation for an open retrospective in the Set the Stage phase. In this phase, you can use the Prime Directive (see section 1.4.6, "The Prime Directive," in Chapter 1) and a collaboratively created team charter to create clear agreements for communication that allow for the exchange of feelings without the potential for any negative consequences. The following are examples of activities that you can use in the first phase to integrate the "soft" topics right from the beginning.

- **The Weather Report:** You display a previously prepared flipchart that the participants can use to record their current mood (sunny, cloudy, rainy, stormy, and so on).
- **Check-In—Draw the Last Sprint:** By drawing their answers, participants respond to questions like "How did you feel during the last iteration?" or "What did you see as the biggest problem?" This activity is based on a blog article by Thorsten Kalnin [1].

- **Check-In—One Question:** The participants take in turns to answer a question like "If you were a car, what car would you be?" or "What kind of pizza was the last iteration?" The funnier the question, the more relaxed the atmosphere.
- **Take a Stand:** Create a scale from "terrible" to "fantastic" on the floor (using masking tape, for example). At the beginning of the retrospective, the participants stand on the scale to show how they feel about the last iteration.

All of these activities take the participants' feelings into account. Of course, a lot of other activities are also suited to this purpose, and I've listed some sources for further activities in Chapter 4, "The Retrospective Facilitator." There are also activities that involve the participants' feelings for the other retrospective phases. In the Gather Data phase, for example, you can have the participants draw the course of their mood beneath a timeline. When were you in a good mood, when in a bad one? The timeline clearly links the participants' moods to the relevant events.

In addition to introducing these special activities, the facilitator's job is also to make sure that an open discussion is possible. I've provided some tips for how to do that in Chapter 1.

Summary

It is quite reasonable to expect that some form of conflict will occur in an agile retrospective, and that is a good thing. Without conflict, there won't be real progress. Your task as a facilitator is to make sure that this conflict is constructive and not destructive. One of the biggest mistakes you can do is to avoid conflict. Avoiding conflict will almost always lead to a smoldering conflict, which can destroy the whole atmosphere in a team. Always address the elephant in the room. This is your job.

In this chapter, you read about different conflicts and pitfalls and how you can cope with them. If you keep them in mind, you will be prepared. If you've read through all chapters of this book, including this one, you have all the knowledge to facilitate successful agile retrospectives. Of course, there will always be something to learn, but this is the whole idea behind retrospectives, right? But now it is up to you to apply this knowledge. This will be a lot of fun. I promise.

Reference

[1] Thorsten Kalnin. 2011. *Draw the Problem.* https://vinylbaustein.net/2011/03/24/draw-the-problem-draw-the-challenge/

11

Change Management

Until now, I have always presented retrospectives as a tool for accompanying a process of continual improvement. That is mostly about making small changes that gradually improve the project process to bring projects to a successful conclusion. Sometimes, though, you don't simply want to make a small change, you want to carry out a large change in the whole organization. That could be the introduction of a new process, the reorganization of the company structure, or other, similar large changes. In these cases, the realization of the change is its own project. Often, a team will be created to make the change a reality. The team's job is to plan and implement the change process. I'm sure that you have participated in a process like this and lived through the implementation of, for example, the ISO 9001 or CMMI or Scrum. Perhaps you are currently in the middle of, or even responsible, for implementing this change. In my experience, such large changes very seldom come off without a hitch and, in most cases, aren't concluded successfully. Sometimes, it seems at first that it will be a success only to later fall back into the old processes. In short, large changes require a lot of time and someone who knows how to implement such a process appropriately.

In this chapter, I show how to effectively set up and carry out such a process with the help of retrospectives. Retrospectives, though, can only define the scope of such a change process and thus help to define what you want. Many books are available specifically on change management, and I can only scratch the surface here. I will, however, pull a few ideas out of those books and suggest some further reading.

11.1 Agile Change Management

As you've learned over the course of this book, the future is very hard to predict. Every organization is a complex, adaptive system with innumerable variables and connections that are hard to grasp. That means that it is seldom possible to create a project plan for a change process that describes all the tasks for the coming months. Instead, it makes more sense to establish a change process that is carried out in a series of iterations, ending each of which by assessing whether you are on the right road or not.

Also, experience has shown that a change process only works when it is carried out simultaneously at all levels. Most change processes are either carried out top-down (initiated and steered by management) or bottom-up (initiated and steered by the workforce) and are thus condemned to failure. Only when everyone understands how the system works and pulls on the same rope can such a process be concluded successfully.

In my view, the following points are indispensable if you want to make sure that a change process will be a success:

- A clear mission/vision that describes the goal of the change process.
- A clear understanding of the organization's current condition. Only if I know where I'm standing now, can I usefully define the next step.
- A broad understanding of change processes in general. How do you implement changes while ensuring that the organization's new condition is stable?
- An iterative process that helps to implement the change step by step.
- Regular reflection that enables you to steer the process effectively and to adapt it when necessary.

11.2 Initiating Change Processes

So, you've decided that you want to change something. This decision is often made because of problems in the organization: bad business numbers, for example, or problems with the implementation of projects. After you've decided on the change, you put together a team whose joint task it is to, for example, make sure that a new process is implemented. For simplicity's sake, I'm just going to assume, in the following pages, that you want to carry out an agile transition in your company. To begin the implementation of this new process, you hold a Kick-Off that represents the start of this initiative. Basing the Kick-Off on the phases of a retrospective will make it easier to carry out.

11.2.1 Set the Stage

Until now, the Set the Stage phase has been used to prepare the ground for a retrospective. In this context, too, you want to prepare the ground for the Kick-Off. You already know how to do this because you can transpose the techniques from regular retrospectives one to one.

The way to put your change into action can be altered several times during the process. What should be seldom changed, however, is the goal to be reached. Starting a change process if you are unclear about the goal makes no sense. This goal is normally represented in the day-to-day project by a clear vision. It shows where you are going with a project and what you want to achieve. A vision is like an especially attractive place on the map that you really want to get to and to which there are many paths. The goal in this first phase of the Kick-Off is to create and clearly define such a vision. It is not only the theme tune for the team working on the change, but it will also help to communicate the goal of the change to the rest of the organization. A good vision is:

- **Clear, concise, and easy to understand:** Avoid long-winded visions full of filler words.
- **Memorable:** The easier the vision is to remember, the better. This also makes communicating the vision easier.

- **Engaging and inspiring:** A good vision should be energizing and speak to peoples' intrinsic motivation.
- **Challenging:** If a vision is too easy to reach, it can't inspire the necessary energy.
- **Both Stable and flexible:** The vision should have a certain flexibility while maintaining a stable core message.
- **Achievable:** Even though your vision is challenging, it should still be achievable.

Here are a few examples of good visions:

- Maintenance-free, disposable plastic watch with a guarantee (this got the Swiss watch industry through the economic crisis).
- "This nation should commit itself to achieving the goal, before the decade is out, of landing a man on the moon and returning him safely to the earth." (Kennedy) [1]
- A computer on every desk and in every home. (Microsoft 1975)
- Our vision is to be earth's most customer-centric company; to build a place where people can come to find and discover anything they might want to buy online. (Amazon)
- A self-sustaining civilization on Mars. (Space X)

Create this vision as a team and make sure that every level of the organization is represented in the discussion. After you have agreed on a vision, the next step is to define the goals that you will need to achieve to realize your dream. Each of these goals should meet the principles of SMART goals (see section 3.5). Prioritizing these goals will then define the first goal of the change process.

The aim of the next step is to find out what skills the team will need to reach this goal. The purpose of the rest of the Kick-Off is to consider these skills because only when the organization has these skills will you be able to reach the goal, which along with the other goals, will realize the vision.

The finished vision, the relevant goals, and the necessary skills will accompany and form the basis of the work of the following months and even years. It goes without saying that the goals might change over time. Some goals might even be dropped, and others added. It is also not unusual to find that, after a certain period, the original vision no longer makes sense. So a vision is no rigid structure, but a flexible and adaptable model as shown in Figure 11-1.

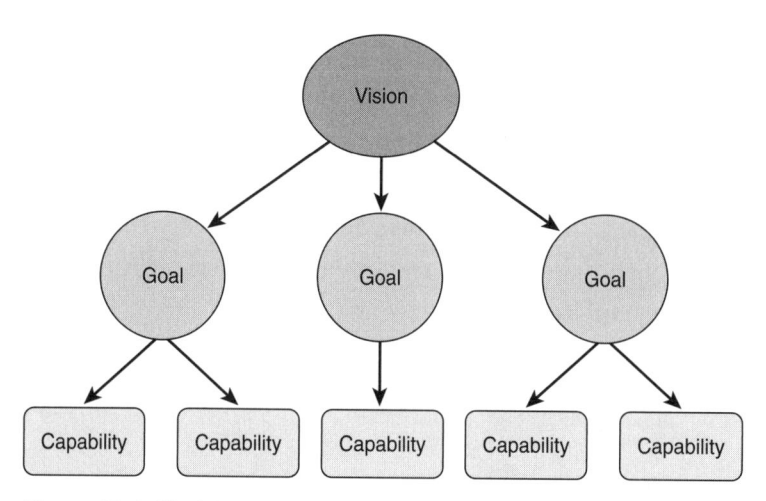

Figure 11-1 Model of the vision

11.2.2 Gather Data

After the goal is clear, it's time to get a grip on reality. After all, a process of change only becomes necessary when an organization isn't capable of reaching its chosen goal. So, the primary objective of this phase is to take stock of the organization's current situation. When you know where you're standing today, you can find out which areas you need to fix first.

To gather this data, you define three areas:

- Organizational structure
- Organizational culture
- Organizational processes

Use a brainstorming session to collect and introduce the characteristics of these three areas. Next, for each area, create a scale from one to ten and use dot voting to determine how well each area is prepared for the coming change. A ten means that the area is ready for the change; a one means that it is still very far from ready. This process gives you an average value for each area that is a good first indicator and that can help as you consider next steps. The lower the value of an area, the higher the risk, either that the necessary changes in this area would be very difficult to implement or that you might be dealing with some very large obstacles. Examples of this could be the missing management buy-in on culture level, or an existing process that impedes you to execute your change. I advise dealing first with the areas of highest risk because this will, from the very beginning, minimize the chances of a failed transition. Of course, it is entirely possible that seemingly simple things can have a large effect, but getting this so-called butterfly effect is not predictable.

With this data in hand, you're ready for the next phase.

11.2.3 Generate Insights

As always, the objective of the Generate Insights phase is to understand both how an organization works and the meaning of the effects that you have observed. Only when you understand what the organization looks like you can consider effective measures of change. You can use the causal loop diagrams (CLDs) described in section 6.2.1 to make the contexts of the organization's system visible. You need to be clear, though: a CLD only ever gives a highly simplified picture of a system. Nevertheless, it is a valuable basis for our experiments in that it does at least show us some possible starting points. A further advantage of a CLD is the very process of its creation. Working as a group to create a CLD can teach you a lot, especially about the mindsets of the people in other areas of the organization. So, it's a way of making yourself see past the end of your own nose.

> **Practical Tip**
> You need to be as realistic as possible when gathering this data. It makes no sense to imagine that the current situation is one thing, only to discover later that it is another. This is another reason why it is important that all levels of the organization be represented in this discussion. Management tends to see things better than they actually are.

A good place to start a CLD is the list of results you have already collected. You can use these results as the variables in the system. For example:

- The skills necessary for achieving our goals
- Potentially, the goals themselves
- The different characteristics of the areas of the organization described earlier (structure, culture, processes)

> **Practical Tip**
> Keep the CLD so that you can use it in coming retrospectives. Of course, you'll need to update it to reflect any new knowledge of the organization.

With the help of the causal loop diagram, you can then depict the variables' relationships to one another, using new variables to fill any holes that appear. This gives you a picture of the system and the relationships within it.

11.2.4 Next Experiments

Now for the most difficult part of the Kick-Off: defining the first experiment. Deciding what you want to do first is not always easy. Thankfully, other people have considered this topic and have provided us with some tools. *Fearless Change*, by Mary Lynn Manns and Linda Rising [2], is a book that stands out from the crowd. In it, Manns and Rising describe 48 patterns that can be used to implement changes in an organization and to make sure that those changes last. The patterns are based on the experiences of a wide variety of people working in change management. They are thus field-tested and of proven value and it is that fact that makes the book so valuable. The patterns are divided into four categories:

- **Continuous:** Patterns that can be used throughout the change process
- **Early:** Patterns that can be used particularly early in the change process
- **Late:** Patterns that are better used late in the change process
- **Resistance:** Patterns that show how to deal with resistance to the envisioned change

In the Kick-Off meeting, you concentrate primarily on the Early category. The next category to consider is Continuous. You take a closer look at Resistance as you encounter any in your organization. Here are a few examples of patterns in the Early category:

- **Ask for Help:** Breathing life into an idea is a hard task. Look for people who can support you.
- **Brown bags:** Use the relaxed atmosphere of the lunch break to introduce your new ideas.
- **E-forum:** Create an internal website or mailing list that people who are interested in your idea can use to find out more.
- **Innovators:** When you begin the process of change, ask for help specifically from those people who like finding and developing new ideas.

- **Be a model:** Use your own ideas, in your own working environment, to experience the advantages and disadvantages firsthand.

- **Customize:** To convince people that the idea is good, you need to adapt it to the needs of your organization.

These patterns can give a team an idea of where to start the process of change. You can use this idea, along with the results of the Kick-Off, to define the first experiment. Calling to mind the SMART acronym can help with this definition.

> **Practical Tip**
>
> The relevant hypotheses are extremely important. These help to establish a goal-oriented process and to adapt the chosen measures (experiments), if the results are other than those you expected (hypotheses). Hypotheses are the core and guide of future work.

11.2.5 Closing

To close the Kick-Off, give a short summary of the whole workshop. This should include answers to the following questions:

- What results were achieved?
- What experiments have been chosen and who is responsible for starting them?
- When do we want to hold the first retrospective and at what interval should they be held in the future?
- Last, but not least, briefly assess the Kick-Off itself by collecting feedback that will help you to run future discussions better. If you like, you can also have the participants fill out a ROTI diagram at the end.

11.3 Accompanying Change Processes

As described earlier, making the change process an iterative one helps you to get a better grasp on the complexity of the organization and the change process itself. That means meeting after one month (at the latest) to assess progress, to adapt the process if necessary, and to define the next experiments. This allows you to steer the process based on empirical evidence and to adapt it quickly if necessary. The goal, though, remains the vision that you defined in the Kick-Off.

Retrospectives were made for this kind of thing! So, it makes sense to accompany the rest of the process with the help of retrospectives.

11.3.1 Set the Stage

Often a good idea when starting a retrospective like this is to find a first indicator of the success of the improvement process: the satisfaction of the team that is itself responsible for the process. You can use different activities to measure this, like the Weather Report or the Check-In (see section 10.6, "Focus on Factual Topics," in Chapter 10). This indicator tells you very quickly whether you're on the right road or whether you're going to be struggling with larger obstacles.

11.3.2 Check Hypotheses

The most important step in a retrospective like this is checking your hypotheses. This is the only way you can really assess whether the experiments that you have carried out so far have had the desired effect. At this moment, have the defined hypotheses become fact and were the relevant experiments successful? Or do you have to admit that a completely different effect has come about? Perhaps there is no perceptible effect at all? At the same time, you have to be aware that not all experiments will have an immediate effect and it may be some time before the results are visible.

To make a long story short: If the desired effect has (still) not been achieved, you have to keep working on it. It makes no sense to tap another keg when those that are already open haven't yet been emptied. Or, still more succinctly: stop starting, start finishing.

The hypotheses that haven't yet been realized are the fodder for the rest of the retrospective.

11.3.3 Gather Data

After you have checked your hypotheses, you again start to collect data in the following areas:

- Organizational structure
- Organizational culture
- Organizational processes

> **Practical Tip**
>
> If some hypotheses haven't been realized, focus the Gather Data phase on collecting all the data that underpin that fact. The question to ask here could go like this: "How do you know that hypothesis A hasn't been realized?" or "What's been missing that would have made hypothesis B a reality?" You could place the data you gather on a timeline to add the chronological component. This data will help you find ideas for experiments in the coming phases.

11.3.4 Generate Insights

Let's say that you have hypotheses that have not yet been realized. In the previous phase, you saw how to recognize that. It is those very things that you now want to look at more closely. You want to understand why they have not been realized and to find the underlying causes.

The causal loop diagram that you used in the Kick-Off will once again come into play. You can now use the data you've gathered and your new experiences to extend the diagram. There will almost certainly be missing variables to be added and further contexts that you had overlooked until now. The overall goal is to build the causes and mechanisms that you gathered before, into your existing causal loop diagram.

This develops your understanding of the system and the internal context of the organization. Sharing these insights with each other is important, as they form the basis of further work.

11.3.5 Define Next Experiments

To develop ideas for new experiments that can help you to realize your hypotheses, you can once more turn to the 48 patterns in Mary Lynn Manns and Linda Rising's book [2]. What pattern haven't you tried yet? What pattern has the potential to help the organization to get the result you need? How can you apply a particular pattern to your own organization?

You can, of course, turn to special models, like the ADKAR or the Five-I models. They also provide starting points for a system.

11.3.5.1 ADKAR Model

The ADKAR model is a goal-oriented model for leading change processes. The acronym stands for:

- **Awareness:** The awareness that you must change something
- **Desire:** The desire to support and be a part of the change
- **Knowledge:** The knowledge of how something can be changed
- **Ability:** The ability to implement the change, step by step, on a daily basis
- **Reinforcement:** The strength to establish the change

This model always involves the people in an organization. You can use the model to find new experiments by asking questions about each of the five elements. For example:

- How can I create, in my organization, the awareness that something needs to change?
- How can I create feelings that motivate people to change? How can I make them want to change?
- What do I have to do to build a concrete idea within the organization of how the change looks? How can I enable my colleagues in the organization to make the change themselves?
- What authority must I grant the people in my network so that they are able to change something?
- What can I do to make people not want to return to the old process?

The answers to these questions can be reformulated as experiments and tried out.

11.3.5.1 Five-I Model

The Five-I model is based on Mark van Vugt's Four-I model. The fifth "I" was added by Jurgen Appelo [3]. The five I's in the model stand for:

- **Information:** Use information radiators to make clear to people the consequences of their current behavior.
- **Identity:** Give people a (cool) identity with which they can identify, like a hip brand.
- **Incentives:** Distribute small rewards for good behavior, like compliments or candy, for example.
- **Infrastructure:** People's behavior is significantly influenced by the tools they use and the infrastructure of their organization.
- **Institutions:** Establish communities of mutual interest within the organization that help to set new standards.

Just as with the ADKAR model, you can find ideas for new experiments by asking questions about each part of the model.

It (almost) doesn't matter which tool you choose as long as you manage to move your change process in the right direction. In the end, your personal situation and the individual context always determine the decision.

11.3.6 Closing

Because retrospectives that are a part of a change process are still also planning tools, answer the following questions collaboratively at the end:

- Which results were worked on?
- Which experiments will be started next and who will be responsible for them?
- When will the next retrospective take place?

Now and then, you should also hold a retrospective on the retrospectives. A continuing improvement process should never neglect the retrospectives themselves.

> **Practical Tip**
> Learn about the different models of change management. These help you find new ideas and explore the available options for developing your change process.

Summary

Change management is no simple task. It can take years for a large change to be fully implemented, especially in larger organizations. So, it's well-nigh impossible to create a comprehensive plan beforehand. Instead, it makes more sense to establish an iterative process that implements the change step by step, and that assesses, at regular intervals, whether you are getting closer to your goal or not. No matter the size of the change, you will never be able to avoid having to adapt the original plan.

Retrospectives are an excellent tool for accompanying change processes. Their clear phase structure provides a frame in which the most important aspects are included:

- What goals are we working toward?
- Where are we today?
- What are the causes of the various behaviors of our organization?
- How can we influence the system to make our changes effective and sustainable?

You must always be clear, however, that retrospectives only provide the frame. They are in no way a substitute for the knowledge of how to establish changes in organizations. Without this additional knowledge, you will have big problems, even if you're using retrospectives to accompany an iterative process. So, you can't get around learning more about the topic of change and becoming familiar with the literature on this topic.

References

[1] John F. Kennedy Presidential Library and Museum. 1961. *Apollo 11 Moon Landing.* https://www.jfklibrary.org/JFK/JFK-Legacy/NASA-Moon-Landing.aspx

[2] Mary L. Manns and Linda Rising. 2005. *Fearless Change: Patterns for Introducing New Ideas.* Pearson Education Inc., Boston, MA.

[3] Jurgen Appelo. 2012. *How to Change the World—Change Management 3.0.* Jojo Ventures BV.

Index

A

ABIDE model, 147–148
  attractors, 148
  barriers, 149
  diversity, 150
  environment, 150–152
ability (ADKAR model), 226
accompanying change processes, 224
  Check Hypothesis phase, 224–225
  Closing phase, 228
  Define Experiments phase, 226–228
    ADKAR model, 226–227
    Five-I model, 227–228
  Gather Data phase, 225
  Generate Insights phase, 225–226
  Set the Stage phase, 224
action, initiating, 172–175
active listening. *See* listening skills
activities
  brainstorming, 50–52
  Check-In, 194, 212
  interactive activities, 185
  Mad, Sad, Glad, 46–48
  sources for, 22–23
    Agile Retrospectives (Derby and Larsen), 23
    Gamestorming, 25–26
    Prime Directive, 26–28
    Retromat, 23–24
    Retrospective Wiki, 24
    Tasty Cupcakes, 24
  Take a Stand, 213
  theme-based activities, 91–93
    kitchen retrospective, 107–111
    orchestra retrospective, 93–99
    pirate retrospective, 111–116
    soccer retrospective, 99–103
    train retrospective, 103–107
  Weather Report, 212
ADKAR model, 226–227
agendas, 40–41
Agerbeck, Brandy, 80–81
Agile change management, 215
  accompanying change processes, 224
    Check Hypothesis phase, 224–225
    Closing phase, 228
    Define Experiments phase, 226–228
    Gather Data phase, 225
    Generate Insights phase, 225–226
    Set the Stage phase, 224
  initiating change processes, 217
    Closing phase, 223
    Define Experiments phase, 221–223
    Gather Data phase, 219–220
    Set the Stage phase, 217–219
  models
    ADKAR, 226–227
    Five-I, 227–228
    Four-I, 227
  requirements for success, 216
  visions, creating, 217–219
Agile Manifesto, 4–6
Agile Retrospectives (Derby and Larsen), 23, 165
agilis, 4
AGM (annual general meeting), 95
Align Constraints technique (Management 3.0 model), 145
alternative approaches
  fortune cookie retrospectives, 196–197
  powerful questions, 198–200
  work retrospectives, 193–196
annual general meeting (AGM), 95
Appelo, Jurgen, 123, 145, 227
attitude of not knowing, 162–163
attractors (ABIDE model), 148
Automattic, 185
awareness (ADKAR model), 226

B

backlogs, sprint, 88
balancing loops, 126–128
barriers (ABIDE model), 149

Berg, Kim, 155, 169. *See also* solution-focused retrospectives
BFTC (Brief Family Therapy Center), 156
black, writing in, 65
block capitals, 66–69
Box, George E. P., 124
brainstorming, 50–52
Brief Family Therapy Center (BFTC), 156

C

car comparison, 45–46
causal loop diagrams (CLDs), 220–221
  balancing loops, 126–128
  constraints, 128–130
  definition of, 125
  delays, 128–130
  example of, 130–132
  opposite effect, 125–126
  reinforcing loops, 126–128
  same effect, 125–126
change management, 215
  accompanying change processes, 224
    Check Hypothesis phase, 224–225
    Closing phase, 228
    Define Experiments phase, 226–228
    Gather Data phase, 225
    Generate Insights phase, 225–226
    Set the Stage phase, 224
  initiating change processes, 217
    Closing phase, 223
    Define Experiments phase, 221–223
    Gather Data phase, 219–220
    Set the Stage phase, 217–219
  models
    ADKAR, 226–227
    Five-I, 227–228
    Four-I model, 227
  requirements for success, 216
  visions, creating, 217–219
change processes
  accompanying, 224
    Check Hypothesis phase, 224–225
    Closing phase, 228
    Define Experiments phase, 226–228
    Gather Data phase, 225
    Generate Insights phase, 225–226
    Set the Stage phase, 224
  initiating, 217
    Closing phase, 223
    Define Experiments phase, 221–223
    Gather Data phase, 219–220
    Set the Stage phase, 217–219
charters, team, 10
Check Hypothesis phase
  change management, 224–225
  explained, 12–13
Check Results step (solution-focused retrospectives), 175–176
Check-In activity, 194, 212
check-in technique, 12
checking hypotheses. *See* Check Hypothesis phase
checking results, 175–176
circular questions, 172
CLDs (causal loop diagrams), 220–221
  balancing loops, 126–128
  constraints, 128–130
  definition of, 125
  delays, 128–130
  example of, 130–132
  opposite effect, 125–126
  reinforcing loops, 126–128
  in retrospectives, 132–136
  same effect, 125–126
Closing phase
  change management
    accompanying change processes, 228
    initiating change processes, 223
  explained, 19–22
  first retrospective, 53
  kitchen retrospective, 111
  Martie—the Management 3.0 model, 147
  orchestra retrospective, 99
  pirate retrospective, 116
  soccer retrospective, 103
  train retrospective, 107
co-facilitators, 181
color of text, 65
common ground, listening for, 63

communication
  emotional feedback questions, 61–62
  encourage technique, 61
  follow-up questions, 59–60
  intended silence, 62–63
  listening for common ground, 63
  paraphrasing, 59
  problem talk versus solution talk, 156–157
  respecting, 58–59
  stacking technique, 60–61
complex systems, 122–124
complexity thinking
  ABIDE model, 147–148
    attractors, 148
    barriers, 149
    diversity, 150
    environment, 150–152
    definition of, 143–152
    Martie—the Management 3.0 model, 144–147
complicated systems, 122–124
confidence, 163–164
conflicting opinions, 202–204
constraints, 128–130
continuous patterns, 222
contradictory opinions, 202–204
cover your ass (CYA) maxim, 211
crayons, filling text boxes with, 70
criteria for goals, 170
CRT (Current Reality Tree), 137–141
CYA (cover your ass) maxim, 211
Cynefin Framework, 122

D

data gathering. *See* Gather Data phase
decision making, 204
Define Experiments phase
  change management
    accompanying change processes, 226–228
    initiating change processes, 221–223
  explained, 17–18
  first retrospective, 50–52
  kitchen retrospective, 111
  Martie—the Management 3.0 model, 147
  orchestra retrospective, 98–99
  pirate retrospective, 115–116
  powerful questions in, 199
  soccer retrospective, 102–103
  train retrospective, 106–107
defining experiments. *See* Define Experiments phase
delays (CLDs), 128–130
Denning, Stephen, 6
Derby, Esther, 9, 23, 165
desire (ADKAR model), 226
Develop Competence technique (Management 3.0 model), 145
diagrams. *See also* ROTI (Return on Time Invested) graph
  CLDs (causal loop diagrams), 220–221
    balancing loops, 126–128
    constraints, 128–130
    definition of, 125
    delays, 128–130
    example of, 130–132
    opposite effect, 125–126
    reinforcing loops, 126–128
    in retrospectives, 132–136
    same effect, 125–126
  fishbone diagram, 114–115
disinterest in improvement, 207–209
distributed retrospectives, 179
  length of, 190
  multiple distributed teams, 179–182
  scattered teams, 185–186
  stacking technique, 190
  teams with singly distributed employees, 183–184
  tips for, 190–191
  tools for, 186–187
    Lino, 189
    Stormz Hangout, 188–189
    Web Whiteboard, 187–188
diversity (ABIDE model), 150
documentation, photo minutes, 87–88
Dot Voting, 7–8
Double Robotics, 183–184
Dräther, Rolf, 121
drawing
  in black, 65
  frames, 66
  rectangles, 68–69
DSDM, 6
dynamic systems, 122

E

early patterns, 222
emotional feedback questions, 61–62
Empower Teams technique
   (Management 3.0 model), 145
encourage technique, 61
Energize People technique
   (Management 3.0 model), 145
environment (ABIDE model), 150–152
events, sorting, 15–16
exceptions, 158
experiments, defining. *See* Define
   Experiments phase
expertise, trusting, 162–163
external facilitators, 85–86

F

facilitators, 2
   characteristics of good facilitator,
      55–57
   co-facilitators, 181
   distributed retrospectives, 185
   external, 85–86
   internal, 81–85
   listening skills
      communication styles, respecting,
         58–59
      emotional feedback questions,
         61–62
      encourage technique, 61
      follow-up questions, 59–60
      intended silence, 62–63
      listening for common ground, 63
      paraphrasing, 59
      stacking technique, 60–61
   photo minutes, 87–88
   visual facilitation, 63–71
      block capitals, 66–69
      color of text, 65
      frames, 66
      letters, writing, 69
      rectangles, drawing, 68–69
      text boxes, 67–68, 70
   visual retrospectives
      force field analysis, 78–80
      perfection game, 76–78
      sources of inspiration for, 80–81
      speedboat retrospective, 71–74
      trading cards, 74–75

*Facilitator's Guide to Participatory
   Decision Making* (Kaner), 57
factual topics, focus on, 210–213
Fearless Change (Manns and Rising),
   221–222
feedback emotion, 61–62
The Fifth Discipline (Senge), 142
filling text boxes, 70
Find Meaning step (solution-focused
   retrospectives), 170–172
finding
   meaning, 170–171
      circular questions, 172
      "What for?," 171–172
   new approaches, 160
first retrospective, 43
   Closing phase, 53
   Define Experiments phase, 50–52
   Gather Data phase, 46–49
   Generate Insights phase, 49–50
   preparation for, 43–45
   Set the Stage phase, 45–46
fishbone diagram, 109–110, 114–115
5-Why method, 7, 49–50
Five-I model, 227–228
flipcharts
   flipchart paper, 38–39
   visual structure, 63–71
      block capitals, 66–69
      color of text, 65
      frames, 66
      letters, writing, 69
      rectangles, drawing, 68–69
      text boxes, 67–68, 70
focus
   on better future, 157–158
   on factual topics, 210–213
   on negative, 209–210
   on strength and skills,
      161–162
follow-up questions, 59–60
food for retrospectives, 39–40
football retrospective. *See* soccer
   retrospective
force field analysis, 78–80
fortune cookie retrospectives,
   196–197
Four-I model, 227
frames, drawing, 66
Frankl, Viktor, 170–171
future, focus on, 157–158

G

games
  perfection game, 76–78
  speedboat retrospective, 71–74
Gamestorming, 25–26
Gather Data phase
  change management
    accompanying change processes, 225
    initiating change processes, 219–220
  explained, 13–16
  first retrospective, 46–49
  kitchen retrospective, 108–109
  Martie—the Management 3.0 model, 146
  orchestra retrospective, 95–96
  pirate retrospective, 113–114
  powerful questions in, 199
  soccer retrospective, 101–102
  train retrospective, 104–105
  work retrospectives, 194
gathering data. *See* Gather Data phase
Generate Insights phase
  change management
    accompanying change processes, 225–226
    initiating change processes, 220–221
  explained, 16–17
  first retrospective, 49–50
  kitchen retrospective, 109–110
  Martie—the Management 3.0 model, 147
  orchestra retrospective, 97–98
  pirate retrospective, 114–115
  train retrospective, 105–106
generating insights. *See* Generate Insights phase
goals. *See also* change management; solution-focused retrospectives
  focus on, 157–158
  precise description of, 156–157
  setting, 167–168
    goal criteria, 170
    "Miracle Question," 169–170
    turning problems into goals, 168–169
  SMART goals, 52, 106–107, 223

The Graphic Facilitator's Guide (Agerbeck), 80–81
graphs, ROTI (Return on Time Invested), 20–21, 53, 116. *See also* diagrams
gray, writing in, 65
Grow Structure technique (Management 3.0 model), 145

H

handwriting, 71
Hanoulle, Yves, 193
heartbeat retrospectives, 32
Herberger, Sepp, 87
Hohmann, Luke, 71
hypotheses
  checking
    change management, 224–225
    explained, 12–13
  definition of, 17–18

I

Improve Everything technique (Management 3.0 model), 145
improvement, disinterest in, 207–209
Initiate Action step (solution-focused retrospectives), 172–175
initiating
  action, 172–175
  change processes, 217
    Closing phase, 223
    Define Experiments phase, 221–223
    Gather Data phase, 219–220
    Set the Stage phase, 217–219
Innovation Games (Hohmann), 71
insights, generating. *See* Generate Insights phase
intended silence, 62–63
interactive activities, 185
internal facilitators, 81–85
Internet Relay Chat (IRC), 185
interventions, 166
  circular questions, 172
  "Miracle Question," 169–170
  scaling, 173–175
  turning problems into goals, 168–169
  "What for?," 171–172

IRC (Internet Relay Chat), 185
iterare, 3
iterations, defining, 3–4

J-K

kaizen culture, 146
Kanban boards, 88
Kaner, Sam, 57
Kerth, Norman, 2, 164
kitchen retrospective, 107
    Closing phase, 111
    Define Experiments phase, 111
    Gather Data phase, 108–109
    Generate Insights phase, 109–110
    Set the Stage phase, 107–108
knowledge
    in ADKAR model, 226
    attitude of not knowing, 162–163
Kua, Pat, 26–27

L

lack of results
    conflicting opinions, 202–204
    indecision, 204
    lack of clear time frame, 205–206
laptops, access to, 181
Larsen, Diana, 9, 23, 165
late patterns, 222
The Leader's Guide to Radical Management (Denning), 6
length of retrospectives
    distributed retrospectives, 190
    solution-focused retrospectives, 176
letters, writing, 69
Lewin, Kurt, 78
Lino, 189
listening for common ground, 63
listening skills
    communication styles, respecting, 58–59
    emotional feedback questions, 61–62
    encourage technique, 61
    follow-up questions, 59–60
    intended silence, 62–63
    listening for common ground, 63
    paraphrasing, 59
    stacking technique, 60–61
location of retrospectives, 34–35
loops. *See* CLDs (causal loop diagrams)

M

Mad, Sad, Glad activity, 46–48
Malik, Fredmund, 170–171
Malik on Management newsletter, 170–171
Management 3.0 (Appelo), 145
Management 3.0 model, 144–147
Manns, Mary Lynn, 221–222
markers, 36–37
Martie—the Management 3.0 model, 144–147
masking tape, 39
materials for retrospectives, 36
    flipchart paper, 38–39
    laptops, 181
    Lino, 189
    markers, 36–37
    online boards, 182, 184, 186
    projectors, 181
    sticky notes, 37–38
    Stormz Hangout, 188–189
    tape, 39
    video conference tools, 181, 184, 186
    Web Whiteboard, 187–188
McCarthy, Jim, 194
McCarthy, Michelle, 194
McCullough, Michael, 24
McGreal, Don, 24
Meadows, Dennis, 125
meaning, finding, 170–171
    circular questions, 172
    "What for?," 171–172
metaphors. *See* theme-based retrospectives
Microsoft Visio, 141
"Miracle Question," 169–170
models. *See also* CLDs (causal loop diagrams)
    ABIDE model, 147–148
        attractors, 148
        barriers, 149
        diversity, 150
        environment, 150–152
    change management
        ADKAR, 226–227
        Five-I, 227–228
        Four-I model, 227
        Martie—the Management 3.0 model, 144–147

Structure-Behaviour Model, 123–124
World3 Model, 125
"Motivation Through Meaning" (Malik), 170–171

N

n–1 rule, 45
negative, focus on, 209–210
network access, 181
new approaches, finding, 160
New Year's Eve Retrospective, 6–8
not knowing, attitude of, 162–163

O

online boards, 182, 184, 186
Open UP, 6
Opening step, 165–167
opinions, conflict of, 202–204
opposite effect (CLDs), 125–126
orchestra retrospective, 93–94
    Closing phase, 99
    Define Experiments phase, 98–99
    Gather Data phase, 95–96
    Generate Insights phase, 97–98
    Set the Stage phase, 94–95

P

painter's tape, 39
pairing, 184
paper
    flipchart paper, 38–39
    sticky notes, 37–38
paraphrasing, 59–60
participants, determining, 32–33
Pasteur, Louis, 42
Pater, Christoph, 38
patience, 163–164
patterns for change management, 221–223
perfection game, 76–78
phases of retrospectives, 8–9
    Check Hypothesis phase
        change management, 224–225
        explained, 12–13
    Closing phase
        change management, 223, 228
        explained, 19–22

first retrospective, 53
kitchen retrospective, 111
Martie—the Management 3.0 model, 147
orchestra retrospective, 99
pirate retrospective, 116
soccer retrospective, 103
train retrospective, 107
Define Experiments phase
    change management, 221–223, 226–228
    explained, 17–18
    first retrospective, 50–52
    kitchen retrospective, 111
    Martie—the Management 3.0 model, 147
    orchestra retrospective, 98–99
    pirate retrospective, 115–116
    powerful questions in, 199
    soccer retrospective, 102–103
    train retrospective, 106–107
Gather Data phase
    change management, 219–220, 225
    explained, 13–16
    first retrospective, 46–49
    kitchen retrospective, 108–109
    Martie—the Management 3.0 model, 146
    orchestra retrospective, 95–96
    pirate retrospective, 113–114
    powerful questions in, 199
    soccer retrospective, 101–102
    train retrospective, 104–105
    work retrospectives, 194
Generate Insights phase
    change management, 220–221, 225–226
    explained, 16–17
    first retrospective, 49–50
    kitchen retrospective, 109–110
    Martie—the Management 3.0 model, 147
    orchestra retrospective, 97–98
    pirate retrospective, 114–115
    soccer retrospective, 102
    train retrospective, 105–106
Set the Stage phase
    change management, 217–219, 224
    explained, 9–12
    first retrospective, 45–46
    kitchen retrospective, 107–108

Martie—the Management 3.0 model, 146
orchestra retrospective, 94–95
pirate retrospective, 112–113
soccer retrospective, 100–101
train retrospective, 103–104
work retrospectives, 194
photo minutes, 87–88
pirate retrospective, 111–112
    Closing phase, 116
    Define Experiments phase, 115–116
    Gather Data phase, 113–114
    Generate Insights phase, 114–115
    Set the Stage phase, 112–113
pitfalls
    conflicting opinions, 202–204
    disinterest in improvement, 207–209
    focus on factual topics, 210–213
    focus on negative, 209–210
    indecision, 205–206
    poor preparation, 201–202
    too many results, 206–207
planning retrospectives, 31. *See also* materials for retrospectives
    agendas, 40–41
    first retrospective, 43–45
    food, 39–40
    participants, 32–33
    time period to be discussed, 31–32
    time/place, 34–35
    topic, 33
poor preparation, 201–202
Positivity (Fredrickson), 165–166
postmortems, 3
powerful questions, 198–200
preparation for retrospectives, 31. *See also* materials for retrospectives
    agendas, 40–41
    distributed retrospectives, 182
    first retrospective, 43–45
    food, 39–40
    participants, 32–33
    poor preparation, 201–202
    time period to be discussed, 31–32
    time/place, 34–35
    topic, 33
Prime Directive, 26–28, 164
problem exceptions, 158
problem talk versus solution talk, 156–157
problems with retrospectives
    conflicting opinions, 202–204
    disinterest in improvement, 207–209
    focus on factual topics, 210–213
    focus on negative, 209–210
    indecision, 204
    lack of clear time frame, 205–206
    poor preparation, 201–202
    too many results, 206–207
    turning into goals, 168–169
Project Retrospectives (Kerth), 2
projectors, 181
punctuality, n-1 rule, 45
Pygmalion effect, 26–27

Q-R

questions
    circular questions, 172
    "Miracle Question," 169–170
    powerful questions, 198–200
    "What for?," 171–172
rectangles, drawing, 68–69
reinforcement (ADKAR model), 226
reinforcing loops, 126–128
repetition of strategies that work, 159
resistance patterns, 222
resources
    sources for visual facilitation, 80–81
    sources of activities, 22–23
        Agile Retrospectives (Derby and Larsen), 23
        Gamestorming, 25–26
        Prime Directive, 26–28
        Retromat, 23–24
        Retrospective Wiki, 24
        Tasty Cupcakes, 24
respecting communication styles, 58–59
results
    checking, 175–176
    documentation of, 87–88
    lack of
        conflicting opinions, 202–204
        lack of clear time frame, 205–206
    too many, 206–207
Retromat, 23–24
retrospectare, 1

Retrospective Wiki, 24
retrospectives. *See also* activities
  Closing phase
    change management, 223, 228
    first retrospective, 53
    kitchen retrospective, 111
    Martie—the Management 3.0 model, 147
    orchestra retrospective, 99
    soccer retrospective, 103
    train retrospective, 107
  compared to postmortems, 3
  Define Experiments phase
    change management, 221–223, 226–228
    first retrospective, 50–52
    kitchen retrospective, 111
    Martie—the Management 3.0 model, 147
    orchestra retrospective, 98–99
    powerful questions in, 199
    soccer retrospective, 102–103
    train retrospective, 106–107
  definition of, 1–6
  distributed, 179
    length of, 190
    multiple distributed teams, 179–182
    scattered teams, 185–186
    stacking technique, 190
    teams with singly distributed employees, 183–184
    tips for, 190–191
    tools for, 186–189
  facilitators, 2
    characteristics of good facilitator, 55–57
    co-facilitators, 181
    distributed retrospectives, 185
    external, 85–86
    internal, 81–85
    listening skills, 58–63
    photo minutes, 87–88
    visual facilitation, 63–71
    visual retrospectives, 71–81
  first retrospective, 43
    Closing phase, 53
    Define Experiments phase, 50–52
    Gather Data phase, 46–49
    Generate Insights phase, 49–50
    preparation for, 43–45
    Set the Stage phase, 45–46
  5-Why method, 7, 49–50
  fortune cookie retrospectives, 196–197
  Gather Data phase
    change management, 219–220, 225
    first retrospective, 46–49
    kitchen retrospective, 108–109
    Martie—the Management 3.0 model, 146
    orchestra retrospective, 95–96
    powerful questions in, 199
    soccer retrospective, 101–102
    train retrospective, 104–105
    work retrospectives, 194
  Generate Insights phase
    change management, 220–221, 225–226
    first retrospective, 49–50
    kitchen retrospective, 109–110
    Martie—the Management 3.0 model, 147
    orchestra retrospective, 97–98
    soccer retrospective, 102
    train retrospective, 105–106
  heartbeat retrospectives, 32
  materials for, 36
    flipchart paper, 38–39
    laptops, 181
    Lino, 189
    markers, 36–37
    online boards, 182, 184, 186
    projectors, 181
    sticky notes, 37–38
    Stormz Hangout, 188–189
    tape, 39
    video conference tools, 181, 184, 186
    Web Whiteboard, 187–188
  New Year's Eve Retrospective, 6–8
  powerful questions, 198–200
  preparation, 31
    agendas, 40–41
    food, 39–40
    materials, 36–39
    participants, 32–33
    poor preparation, 201–202
    time period to be discussed, 31–32
    time/place, 34–35
    topic, 33

prime directive of, 164
Set the Stage phase
  change management, 217–219, 224
  first retrospective, 45–46
  kitchen retrospective, 107–108
  Martie—the Management 3.0 model, 146
  orchestra retrospective, 93–95
  soccer retrospective, 100–101
  train retrospective, 103–104
  work retrospectives, 194
solution-focused approach, 156
  attitude of not knowing, 162–163
  focus on better future, 157–158
  focus on strength and skills, 161–162
  new approaches, finding, 160
  patience and confidence, 163–164
  prime directive of retrospectives, 164
  problem exceptions, 158
  problem talk versus solution talk, 156–157
  repetition of strategies that work, 159
  scaling, 161
solution-focused retrospectives, 155–156, 165
  Check Results step, 175–176
  Find Meaning step, 170–172
  Initiate Action step, 172–175
  length of, 176
  Opening step, 165–167
  Set Goals step, 167–170
systemic retrospectives, 119–120
  complexity thinking, 143–152
  system thinking, 124–143
  systems, 120–124
theme-based retrospectives, 91–93
  kitchen retrospective, 107–111
  orchestra retrospective, 93–99
  pirate retrospective, 111–116
  soccer retrospective, 99–103
  train retrospective, 103–107
time limits, 48
typical problems and pitfalls
  conflicting opinions, 202–204
  disinterest in improvement, 207–209
  focus on factual topics, 210–213

  focus on negative, 209–210
  lack of clear time frame, 205–206
  poor preparation, 201–202
  too many results, 206–207
visual retrospectives
  force field analysis, 78–80
  perfection game, 76–78
  sources of inspiration for, 80–81
  speedboat retrospective, 71–74
  trading cards, 74–75
  work retrospectives, 193–196
Return on Time Invested. *See* ROTI (Return on Time Invested) graph
Rhode, Mike, 81
Rising, Linda, 221–222
role changes, 84–85
rooms for retrospectives, 34–35
Rosenthal effect, 26–27
ROTI (Return on Time Invested) graph, 20–21, 53, 116

S

Sahota, Michael, 24
same effect (CLDs), 125–126
scaling, 161, 173–175
scattered teams, 185–186
Scrum, 6
  sprint backlog, 88
  sprints, 3
self-adhesive film, 37–38
self-fulfilling prophesy, 26–27
Senge, Peter, 142
Set Goals step (solution-focused retrospectives), 167–168
Set the Stage phase
  change management
    accompanying change processes, 224
    initiating change processes, 217–219
  explained, 9–12
  first retrospective, 45–46
  kitchen retrospective, 107–108
  Martie—the Management 3.0 model, 146
  orchestra retrospective, 94–95
  pirate retrospective, 112–113
  soccer retrospective, 100–101

train retrospective, 103–104
work retrospectives, 194
setting goals, 167–168
  goal criteria, 170
  "Miracle Question," 169–170
  turning problems into goals, 168–169
setting the stage. *See* Set the Stage phase
Shazer, Steve de, 155. *See also* solution-focused retrospectives
Sibbet, Daniel, 80
sides, drawing, 68–69
silence, intended, 62–63
sístima, 120–121
The Sketchnote Handbook (Rhode), 81
skills, focus on, 161–162
SMART goals, 52, 106–107, 223
snacks for retrospectives, 39–40
Snowden, David, 122
soccer retrospective, 99–100
  Closing phase, 103
  Define Experiments phase, 102–103
  Gather Data phase, 101–102
  Generate Insights phase, 102
  Set the Stage phase, 100–101
solution talk, 156–157
solution-focused approach, 156. *See also* solution-focused retrospectives
  attitude of not knowing, 162–163
  focus on better future, 157–158
  focus on strength and skills, 161–162
  new approaches, finding, 160
  patience and confidence, 163–164
  prime directive of retrospectives, 164
  problem exceptions, 158
  problem talk versus solution talk, 156–157
  repetition of strategies that work, 159
  scaling, 161
solution-focused retrospectives, 155–156
  solution-focused approach, 156
    attitude of not knowing, 162–163
    focus on better future, 157–158
    focus on strength and skills, 161–162
    new approaches, finding, 160
    patience and confidence, 163–164

prime directive of retrospectives, 164
problem exceptions, 158
problem talk versus solution talk, 156–157
repetition of strategies that work, 159
scaling, 161
steps of, 165
  Check Results step, 175–176
  Find Meaning step, 170–172
  Initiate Action step, 172–175
  length of, 176
  Opening step, 165–167
  Set Goals step, 167–170
sorting events, 15–16
speedboat retrospective, 71–74
sprint backlog, 88
sprints, 3, 88
stacking technique, 60–61, 190
stage, setting. *See* Set the Stage phase
Standup meetings, 176
static systems, 122
sticky notes, 37–38
Stormz Hangout, 188–189
strength, focus on, 161–162
Structure-Behaviour Model, 123–124
Super Stickies, 37–38
supplies for retrospectives, 36
  flipchart paper, 38–39
  laptops, 181
  Lino, 189
  markers, 36–37
  online boards, 182, 184, 186
  projectors, 181
  sticky notes, 37–38
  Stormz Hangout, 188–189
  tape, 39
  video conference tools, 181, 184, 186
  Web Whiteboard, 187–188
supporting participants, 59–60
system thinking
  CLDs (causal loop diagrams)
    balancing loops, 126–128
    constraints, 128–130
    definition of, 125
    delays, 128–130
    example of, 130–132

opposite effect, 125–126
reinforcing loops, 126–128
in retrospectives, 132–136
same effect, 125–126
CRT (Current Reality Tree), 137–141
definition of, 124–125
limitations of, 142–143
systemic retrospectives, 119–120
complex systems, 122–124
complexity thinking
ABIDE model, 147–152
definition of, 143–152
Martie—the Management 3.0 model, 144–147
complicated systems, 122–124
system thinking
CLDs (causal loop diagrams), 125–136
CRT (Current Reality Tree), 137–141
definition of, 124–125
limitations of, 142–143
systems
definition of, 120–122
dynamic systems, 122
static systems, 122
systems. *See also* system thinking
complex systems, 122–124
complicated systems, 122–124
definition of, 120–124
dynamic systems, 122
static systems, 122

T

Take a Stand activity, 213
tape, 39
tardiness, n-1 rule, 45
Tasty Cupcakes, 24
TDD (test-driven development), 119
team charters, 10
teams
definition of, 15
distributed
multiple distributed teams, 179–182
scattered teams, 185–186
teams with singly distributed employees, 183–184

pairing, 184
team charters, 10
test-driven development (TDD), 119
text
block capitals, 66–69
color of, 65
letters, writing, 69
text boxes, 67–68, 70
text boxes, 67–68, 70
theme-based retrospectives, 91–93
kitchen retrospective, 107
Closing phase, 111
Define Experiments phase, 111
Gather Data phase, 108–109
Generate Insights phase, 109–110
Set the Stage phase, 107–108
orchestra retrospective, 93–94
Closing phase, 99
Define Experiments phase, 98–99
Gather Data phase, 95–96
Generate Insights phase, 97–98
Set the Stage phase, 93–95
pirate retrospective, 111–112
Closing phase, 116
Define Experiments phase, 115–116
Gather Data phase, 113–114
Generate Insights phase, 114–115
Set the Stage phase, 112–113
soccer retrospective, 99–100
Closing phase, 103
Define Experiments phase, 102–103
Gather Data phase, 101–102
Generate Insights phase, 102
Set the Stage phase, 100–101
train retrospective, 103
Closing phase, 107
Define Experiments phase, 106–107
Gather Data phase, 104–105
Generate Insights phase, 105–106
Set the Stage phase, 103–104
thinking
complexity thinking
ABIDE model, 147–152
definition of, 143–152
Martie—the Management 3.0 model, 144–147

system thinking
    CLDs (causal loop diagrams), 125–136
    CRT (Current Reality Tree), 137–141
    definition of, 124–125
    limitations of, 142–143
time
    clear time frame, 205–206
    lack of, 209
    time limits, 48
    time period to be discussed, 31–32
    time/place for retrospectives, 34–35
Time Timer clock, 48
timelines, 14
too many results, 206–207
tools. *See also* materials for retrospectives
    Lino, 189
    Stormz Hangout, 188–189
    Web Whiteboard, 187–188
topic, determining, 33
Toyota, Sakichi, 7
trading cards, 74–75
train retrospective, 103
    Closing phase, 107
    Define Experiments phase, 106–107
    Gather Data phase, 104–105
    Generate Insights phase, 105–106
    Set the Stage phase, 103–104
Treasure, Julian, 57
trusting expertise, 162–163
turning problems into goals, 168–169

U-V

video conference tools, 181, 184, 186
visions, creating, 217–219

visual facilitation, 63–71
    block capitals, 66–69
    color of text, 65
    frames, 66
    letters, writing, 69
    rectangles, drawing, 68–69
    text boxes, 67–68, 70
Visual Meetings (Sibbet), 80
visual retrospectives
    force field analysis, 78–80
    perfection game, 76–78
    sources of inspiration for, 80–81
    speedboat retrospective, 71–74
    trading cards, 74–75
visualization, timelines, 14
Vugt, Mark van, 227

W

Weather Report, 212
Web Whiteboard, 187–188
websites
    Retromat, 23–24
    Retrospective Wiki, 24
    Tasty Cupcakes, 24
wedge-tipped markers, 36
Weisbart, Adam, 196
"What for?" question, 171–172
Work phase (work retrospectives), 195
work retrospectives, 193–196
working agreement, 10
World3 Model, 125
writing
    in black, 65
    in text boxes, 67–68

X-Y-Z

XNote Stopwatch for Windows, 48
XP, 6

REGISTER YOUR PRODUCT at informit.com/register
Access Additional Benefits and SAVE 35% on Your Next Purchase

- Download available product updates.
- Access bonus material when applicable.
- Receive exclusive offers on new editions and related products.
  (Just check the box to hear from us when setting up your account.)
- Get a coupon for 35% for your next purchase, valid for 30 days. Your code will be available in your InformIT cart. (You will also find it in the Manage Codes section of your account page.)

Registration benefits vary by product. Benefits will be listed on your account page under Registered Products.

InformIT.com—The Trusted Technology Learning Source

InformIT is the online home of information technology brands at Pearson, the world's foremost education company. At InformIT.com you can
- Shop our books, eBooks, software, and video training.
- Take advantage of our special offers and promotions (informit.com/promotions).
- Sign up for special offers and content newsletters (informit.com/newsletters).
- Read free articles and blogs by information technology experts.
- Access thousands of free chapters and video lessons.

Connect with InformIT–Visit informit.com/community
Learn about InformIT community events and programs.

informIT.com
the trusted technology learning source

Addison-Wesley • Cisco Press • IBM Press • Microsoft Press • Pearson IT Certification • Prentice Hall • Que • Sams • VMware Press

ALWAYS LEARNING   PEARSON